Chairs

Published in 2012 by New Holland Publishers (UK) Ltd
London • Cape Town • Sydney • Auckland
www.newhollandpublishers.com
Garfield House, 86–88 Edgware Road, London W2 2EA, United Kingdom
Wembley Square First Floor Solan Road Gardens Cape Town 8001 South Africa
Unit 1, 66 Gibbes Street, Chatswood, NSW 2067, Australia
218 Lake Road, Northcote, Auckland, New Zealand

10 9 8 7 6 5 4 3 2 1

A catalogue record for this book is available from the British Library

ISBN: 978 1 78009 061 0

Publisher: Aruna Vasudevan
Senior Editor: Jolyon Goddard
Cover and Inside Design: Colin Hall
Production: Melanie Dowland
Picture Editor: Susannah Jayes
Printer: Toppan Leefung Printing Ltd (China)

Chairs
20th-Century Classics

NEW HOLLAND

Chairs: 20th-Century Classics showcases almost 100 of the most desirable and iconic objects in this area. This is by no means meant to be a directory of 20th-century chairs – we leave that to other people and other books – but is rather a personal selection of those chairs, stools and chaises longues that we feel are most desirable, influential, inspirational and, quite simply, are first among equals.

Chairs mixes museum classics – items featured in such places as the Museum of Modern Art (MoMA) in New York and the Design Museum or Victoria and Albert Museum (V&A) in London – with pieces that are relatively easy to purchase. It provides, we hope, useful insight into a wealth of beautiful and inspiring 20th-century design classics.

For ease of use this book is arranged chronologically within 10 colour-coded sections, each representing a decade. In some cases the exact year of creation has been surprisingly difficult to pinpoint as sources vary; in such instances we have chosen to cite the date used in the most credible sources available. Each entry features a beautiful photograph, often kindly supplied by the manufacturer or designer, an informative and lively essay putting the object and designer in context, some top tips on what to look out for and at least one website relating to the chair under discussion.

We hope this book introduces you to some of the best 20th-century chairs – including items that can be found on your doorstep – and to the extraordinary men and women who created them, such as Marcel Breuer, Arne Jacobsen, Robin Day, Charles and Ray Eames, Hans J. Wegner, Joe Colombo, Ron Arad and Eileen Gray.

Finally, we would like to thank Aruna Vasudevan, our Publisher, for commissioning this book and for her insight and advice in selecting the entries; Colin Hall, the designer; Susannah Jayes, the picture editor – and the many manufacturers and industrial designers who have provided much needed advice and information.

– Fletcher Sibthorp and Scala Quin

Contents

1940s

1950s

1960s

High Back Chair for Miss Cranston's Tea Rooms
Charles Rennie Mackintosh

Scottish architect and designer Charles Rennie Mackintosh produced some of the most innovative designs of the early 20th century. This is one of his best-known chairs.

Mackintosh, his wife, Margaret Macdonald, and sister- and brother-in-law Frances Macdonald and James Herbert MacNair, were leading exponents of the Glasgow Style, which became so influential at the turn of the 20th century. Mackintosh was exalted for his striking, rectilinear designs, which drew on Japanese aesthetics and utilized natural materials. Mackintosh was commissioned by Miss Catherine Cranston in about 1896 to design some murals for one of her tea rooms. This high-backed chair sat in 205 Ingram Street. It is an elongated version of an earlier dining chair that had a single pierced square in the central back splats. The High Back Chair has three extra pierced squares at the top of each of the central back splats. The original chairs were stained dark brown oak to contrast with the airy interiors, but the original design shows that they were intended to be stained green.

☞ Items to look out for
Original chairs are rare. They can be seen in museums globally.

⚱ Top Tips
Freud Ltd makes this chair to the original specifications in solid European oak, with removable seat pads covered in unbleached calico. A chair costs about £450 (US $750).

▥ Websites
Charles Rennie Mackintosh Society
www.crmsociety.com
Freud Ltd
www.freud.eu

Stuhl Chair (Model 209)
August Thonet

The celebrated architect Le Corbusier used the model 209 chair, better known as the Wiener Stuhl Chair, in many of his buildings. He called it a piece of great 'nobility'.

Architect August Thonet designed the Stuhl Chair in 1904. It has been praised by designers and the public since then. Its minimalist simplicity and elegance are typical of the Viennese Gebrüder Thonet company's designs. It still manufactures the chair today.

Like the father of all bentwood chairs, Model No. 214 (also known as the 'Vienna Coffee House Chair') which was designed by Gebrüder Thonet founder Michael Thonet in the 1850s, the Stuhl Chair is made up of six pieces. Its genius rests in the back piece and back legs of the steamed bentwood, which are moulded almost sculpturally from one piece of solid beechwood.

Paying tribute to August Thonet's Stuhl Chair, acclaimed French architect and industrial designer Le Corbusier declared, 'Never has anything been created more elegant and better in its conception, more precise in its execution, and more excellently functional'.

Items to look out for

The original chair has a back section and back legs made from one piece of solid moulded beech.

Top Tips

Reproductions are available in several colours with different styles of seat. Plywood seat £459 (US $709); cane seat £486 (US $761); perforated plywood seat £470 (US $736); upholstered seat and back, fabric £619 (US $970); upholstered seat and back, leather £747 (US $1,174).

Websites

TwentyTwentyone
www.twentytwentyone.com

Sitzmaschine
Josef Hoffmann

Found in leading design collections around the world, Josef Hoffmann's Sitzmaschine ('machine for sitting') was originally designed for the Purkersdorf Sanatorium in Vienna.

Josef Hoffmann was a great admirer of Charles Rennie Mackintosh; he believed that Mackintosh's work was both forward-thinking and beautifully crafted. Architect Hoffmann helped found the influential Wiener Werkstätte in Vienna, which was influenced by the English Arts and Crafts Movement. As one of the first commissions for the Werkstätte, Hoffmann undertook to design the exterior and furnishings of the Purkersdorf Sanatorium in Vienna. His 'Sitzmaschine' pays more than a nod to Philip Webb's Arts and Crafts Morris Chair (1866). It also illustrates how innovations in construction techniques were filtering through to commercial design. The reclining chair's exposed and streamlined form is made up of bent-beechwood curves and a back panel of sycamore pierced with open geometric grids. The rows of knobs on the adjustable back combine both functional and decorative elements that are typical of the Viennese Werkstätte style.

☞ **Items to look out for**

The original chairs are hard to find but one came up at Christie's recently and sold for £15,151 (US $23,750).

Top Tips

J & J Kohn produced several different versions of the Sitzmaschine, some with cushioned seat and backrest, until 1916.

Be careful to check listings carefully. Vitra makes a miniature version of the chair for about £200 (US $313) – considerably less than the auction price listed above.

Websites
MoMA
www.moma.org

Faaborg Chair
Kaare Klint

Danish architect Kaare Klint produced many famous and influential designs. He received international recognition for the Faaborg Chair.

Kaare Klint is, for many people, the true father of Danish design. In 1924, Klint was one of the driving forces in the founding of the Furniture School at Copenhagen's Royal Academy of Fine Arts, where he also taught such creative geniuses as Poul Kjærholm. He believed in thoroughly researching any project that he undertook so that it would be designed to best fit the task for which it was meant, while also being beautifully crafted and attractive to look at. The Faaborg Chair was conceived in 1914 as part of the commission that he and mentor Calle Peterson undertook to design the furniture and fittings for the Faaborg Museum. The brief – to create a light and easy chair that could be placed by visitors in front of any painting they wanted to look at – was fully met. Drawing on classical lines, the Faaborg Chair has a curved back that was originally produced in French rattan, as was the seat. From 1964 onwards, it was made with a fixed seat cushion.

☞ **Items to look out for**

The original chair was produced with a French rattan seat and back. A modern mahogany or European cherry version with an oxhide seat can cost £3,939 (US $6,352).

🍸 **Top Tips**

Rud Rasmussen has manufactured the chair since 1931.

If you buy a chair with a fixed cushioned seat in Niger leather, oxhide or fabric, it will have been made after 1964.

www **Websites**
Rud Rasmussen
www.rudrasmussen.com

Red/Blue Chair
Gerrit Thomas Rietveld

While a member of the Amsterdam-based De Stijl group, which included artist Piet Mondrian, Gerrit Thomas Rietveld produced the acclaimed Red/Blue Chair.

Dutch architect and furniture maker Gerrit Thomas Rietveld first developed the design for an unpainted armchair based on geometric principles in 1917–18. The design was the prototype for what would become – in its painted form – the Red/Blue Chair and it was a realization of the Amsterdam-based De Stijl movement's principles. Rietveld sought to create spiritual harmony through the merging of geometry and primary colours. The Red/Blue Chair was one of the first examples of the application of this philosophy in a three-dimensional form. Rietveld originally painted it in grey, black and white, but after seeing fellow De Stijl member Piet Mondrian's abstract red, blue, yellow and black paintings he repainted it in those colours. Rietveld intended it to be produced for the mass market and so kept the design simple. The chair created a sensation when it was first shown and it has since become an iconic piece of 20th-century design.

☞ **Items to look out for**

This chair is in major design collections, such as MoMA.

The chair was intended for mass production so the original pieces of wood were standard lumber lengths for the time.

🍴 **Top Tips**

Cassina makes a stained beech version for about £1,660 (US $2,602). A maple self-assembly kit, supplied with the original design and Gorilla Glue is also available for £65 (US $149).

Websites
Cassina
www.cassina.com

See also
■ Zig-Zag Chair, p50

B3 (Wassily Chair)
Marcel Breuer

Marcel Breuer developed the B3 Chair while he was head of the carpentry workshop at the celebrated Bauhaus. The chair is more popularly known as the 'Wassily Chair'.

The seamless tubular steel of the Adler bicycle that Marcel Breuer rode around Dessau in Germany inspired him to develop a range of furniture from the same material. That wish, combined with the desire to design a chair supported by a single base – a cantilever chair – led to the B3. Both functional and comfortable, Breuer's chair was also stylish and modern. The original was made for just a few years before the outbreak of the Second World War in 1939. However, in the consumer boom following the war, well-designed, mass-market furniture was in demand and the B3 was manufactured by Gavina in Bologna, Italy, and distributed through Stendig. Now marketed as the 'Wassily Chair' (artist Wassily Kandinsky received an early prototype made of canvas (or wire-mesh) fabric straps with a bent nickelled-steel frame), the straps were replaced by black leather and the frame made of chrome-plated steel. In 1968, Knoll bought Gavina and the 'Wassily' name, but the design patent had expired.

☞ **Items to look out for**

Original B3 models, made of canvas straps and nickelled steel, are rare.

A **'licensed product'** will have the Knoll stamp.

♦ **Top Tips**

More modern versions are made of leather and chrome-plated steel.

Gavina-produced Wassily Chairs still exist but most chairs are Knoll-produced (£1,250/US $2,000). Cheaper versions can be found for about £310 (US $500).

💻 **Websites**

Knoll
www.knoll.com

See also

■ B32 p29

Cantilever Chair (S33)
Mart Stam

If the courts are to be believed, the race to design a cantilever chair was lost by Marcel Breuer to Dutch architect Mart Stam, who designed the S33 in the mid-1920s.

Mart Stam, like Breuer, was experimenting with tubular steel in his designs in the 1920s. In 1925, he is believed to have devised a chair without any back legs. It relied on a single twisted piece of steel pipe to counterbalance the weight of the person sitting on it. The chair, the S33, was only produced in 1927 in Stuttgart's Weissenhof-Siedlung, but Stam's design is considered to be the first workable manifestation of a cantilever chair, a concept that would revolutionize 20th-century furniture design. Perhaps foreseeing this, Stam and Breuer went to court between 1926 and 1932 over the matter of copyright – which Stam eventually won.

The S33 comprises a tubular steel form with a saddle-leather seat and back. Stam developed his design by experimenting with gas pipes connected with flanges. He initially concentrated on the clarity of form rather than on the chair's flexibility, something which led critics to comment that the S33 was both rigid and uncomfortable.

☞ **Items to look out for**

The earliest form of Stam's chair had a horizontal bar between the front legs. This was replaced by supports under the seat.

🍷 **Top Tips**

Thonet manufactures the S33, based on Stam's original design, in classic leather and with a meshed back. It retails at about £225 (US $352).

S34 – the version with armrests is also available.

💻 **Websites**
Thonet
www.thonet.de

Transat Chair
Eileen Gray

Anglo–Irish designer Eileen Gray was a pioneer of the modernist movement. She designed the Transat ('Transatlantic') Chair for the E-1027 villa near Monaco.

A successful female designer working in a world dominated by men such as Le Corbusier, Eileen Gray is often underrated both as a designer and architect (although she wasn't formally trained as the latter). Gray gained a great reputation as a lacquer artist in London and Paris and was also one of the first designers to experiment with tubular steel in furniture. In the 1920s and '30s she collaborated on a number of projects with her sometime lover Romanian architect Jean Badovici. Gray designed her two most famous chairs – the Transat and Bibendum – for E-1027, the house that she and Badovici built in Roquebrune near Monaco.

Said to be inspired by ocean liner deckchairs, the Transat comprised a suspended panel of cushioned leather topped by a pivoting headrest on a sycamore frame with exposed chrome-plated mounts. It was many years before the Transat could be commercially produced and there were several early prototypes.

☞ Items to look out for
A maple chair from 1927 recently was sold at auction for £129,895 (US $193,000).

⚬ Top Tips
A modern version costs about £2,387 (US $3,744) and can be bought in a range of woods.

▭ Websites
Bonluxat
www.bonluxat.com

See also
■ Bibendum Chair, p32

Chaise Longue LC4
Le Corbusier/Jeanneret/Perriand

The Chaise Longue LC4 was designed to evoke the shape and comfort of an 18th-century daybed. Today, it is viewed as a design classic.

In 1929, **Charles-Édouard Jeanneret-Gris** (better known as Le Corbusier), his cousin Pierre Jeanneret and the architect Charlotte Perriand unveiled the Chaise Longue LC4 at the Salon d'Automne in Paris. The LC4 was all about style and comfort.The design has three main parts: a high-grade steel-coated base, a curved chrome-plated frame and a cushioned/padded leather mat with a headrest. The frame is adjustable, allowing the user to assume a variety of poses, from fully reclining to that of being upright. The chair's upholstered seat pad was in black leather, although today a variety of fabrics and colours are available. The design of the LC4 came to epitomize what became known as International Style. The chaise was produced from the late 1920s until the late 1950s. Le Corbusier, in collaboration with Swiss designer Heidi Weber, modified the design in 1959. The most significant adaptation was that the elliptical tube base was replaced with a more readily available oval tube structure.

☞ Items to look out for

The original has an elliptical tube base with black leather upholstery.

🍖 Top Tips

Italian company Cassina has the official licence to produce the LC4; it retails at about £3,125 (US $5,000) and measures 56.4x160cm (22.2x63in). The frame is stamped with Le Corbusier's signature. The base is always black.

A faux LC4 retails at about £600 (US $960).

🌐 Websites

Cassina
www.cassina.com

See also

◼ LC2 (Grand Confort) Club Chair, p30

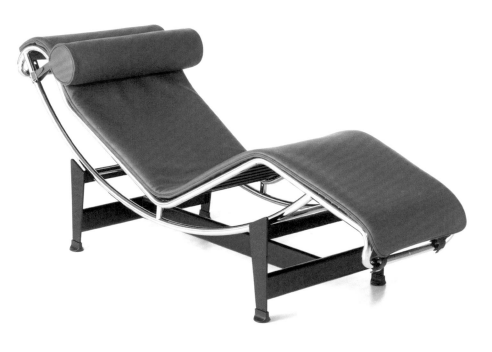

B32
Marcel Breuer

The B32 is arguably the most perfect execution of an early cantilever chair. Its designer, Hungarian-born Marcel Breuer was one of the leading exponents of modernism.

A protegé of Walter Gropius and trained in Bauhaus principles, Marcel Breuer believed in clear, classic designs that were also functional. Hungarian-born Breuer experimented with cantilever mechanisms and tubular steel throughout the 1920s, and while doing so designed several iconic chairs – and became involved in a lawsuit with Mart Stam.

While the B3 showed the possibilities of tubular steel in furniture design, the B32, or Cesca Side Chair, which he designed before his architectural career really took off, is probably one of the most influential chairs of this early period and certainly one that has been copied by designers many times since.

The long lengths of exposed tubular steel provide the chair's structure and industrial feel. However, the latter is somewhat softened by Breuer's use of woven wicker and beech on the back support and seat, which serves to merge the more traditional materials with the more industrial.

 Items to look out for

The original B32 is made of tubular steel and cane and beech

If you're buying a 'licensed product' look for the Knoll stamp and Breuer's signature on the bottom.

Top Tips

More modern versions retail without arms from £412 (US $646); with arms from £514 (US $807).

 Websites

Knoll
www.knoll.com

See also

■ B3, p20
■ Isokon Long Chair, p54

LC2 (Grand Confort) Club Chair
Le Corbusier/Jeanneret/Perriand

1928

The LC2, along with the LC3, is a design classic. It is a stunning example of the collaboration between geniuses Le Corbusier, Jeanneret and Perriand.

The LC2 is among the finest examples of modernist furniture and was the result of the collaboration between designer Charlotte Perriand, Swiss/ French architect and designer Le Corbusier and his cousin, Pierre Jeanneret. Le Corbusier wanted to conceive three chairs with chromium steel-plated bottoms for two of the projects that they were working on – the Maison La Roche in Paris and a garden pavilion of an American couple, Henry and Barbara Church. The B301 Sling was designed for 'conversation'; the B306 Chaise Longue for sleeping and the boxy and overstuffed LC2 for relaxation.

Recognizable for its geometric form, which mixes leather and tubular steel, the LC2 was a response to the more traditional club armchair. It was deemed uncomfortable by critics of the time, but today is considered to be a style icon. It combines the industrial rationale and elegant minimalism of International Style with ultimate comfort.

☞ **Items to look out for**
The LC2 is more compact in design than the LC3.

🍃 **Top Tips**
More modern versions are made of aniline leather and highly polished tubular stainless steel frames.

If you're buying a licensed product, look for the Cassina stamp.

Modern versions retail at about £680 (US $1,065).

🌐 **Websites**
Cassina
www.cassina.com

See also
■ Chaise Longue LC4, p26

Bibendum Chair
Eileen Gray

As well as the Transat Chair, Eileen Gray is thought to have designed the Bibendum Chair for the L-shaped E-1027 villa in Monaco. It is one of her most recognizable designs.

Although Eileen Gray was a highly influential designer of the modernist style, her work was largely forgotten until the 1970s, when an auction brought many of her forgotten pieces to light. The Bibendum Chair was one such piece of furniture and its popularity led it to be brought back into production. It is today licensed worldwide by Aram.

Showing Gray's expertise with tubular steel, the Bibendum was so named by Gray because of its more than passing resemblance to the character used by Michelin to advertise its tyres. Comprising a chrome tubular frame, the chair combines comfort with industrial form in its blending of oversized cushions, steel and leather. The back is made up of two leather-covered tyre-shaped semi-circular cushions that lie on a cushioned seat pad with a beechwood and mesh frame over a tubular base. Whether the chair was designed for the E-1027 villa or for Madame Mathieu Lévy's Parisian apartment as is also claimed, it is a classic.

☞ **Items to look out for**

The licensed product is made by Aram and retails at about £3,300 (US $5,218).

Top Tips

More modern versions are available in an array of colours.

There are many unlicensed chairs available for as little as £200 (US $314).

Websites

Aram
www.aram.co.uk

See also

■ Transat Chair, p24

Barcelona Chair
Mies van der Rohe/Reich

The Barcelona Chair can be seen everywhere – in offices and homes around the world. It is probably Mies van der Rohe and Reich's most recognized design.

The chair is the product of a collaboration between acclaimed architect Ludwig Mies van der Rohe and interior designer Lilly Reich during the 1920s. It was originally attributed solely to Mies van der Rohe, but in recent years Reich's contribution to the chair's design has been acknowledged.

In 1929, the couple designed the low, tilted chair for the German Pavilion at the International Exposition in Barcelona. The Pavilion mixed marble, brass, glass and travertine to great effect and the Barcelona Chair's steel and leather thronelike design fitted it admirably. The frame was originally designed to be bolted together and had an expensive pigskin-leather finish on the pads.

The chair was produced in limited quantities from the 1930s to '50s. In 1950 it was redesigned to incorporate a seamless stainless steel frame and bovine leather replaced the pigskin. In 1953, Knoll acquired van der Rohe's rights. It still manufactures the chair to this day.

☞ **Items to look out for**
The original chairs combined reflective chrome with ivory pigskin.

♀ **Top Tips**
There are so many copies on the market today. The licensed Knoll version sells for upwards of £2,500 (US $4,000).

The Knoll version has a Knoll Studio logo and Mies van der Rohe's signature stamped into the frame.

🌐 **Websites**
Knoll
www.knoll.com

See also
■ Brno Chair, p36

Brno Chair (MR50)
Mies van der Rohe/Reich

A 20th-century design classic, the Brno Chair (MR50) was named one of the '80 greatest man-made treasures of the world' by English architecture guru Dan Cruikshank in 2005.

The MR50 is a modernist cantilever chair. It was designed by German-born architect Ludwig Mies van der Rohe in collaboration with German designer Lilly Reich in 1929–30 as bedroom furniture for the Tugendhat House in Brno, now in present-day Czech Republic. It has come to be known more popularly as the 'Brno Chair'. Influenced by the chairs of Dutch architect and designer Mart Stam, Mies van der Rohe and Reich combined clean, clear lines with comfort in the MR50. The original chair frame was made from a single piece of stainless steel that curved round into a C-shape forming the arms and legs. The steel frame was also bent under the seat to form the cantilever. An elegant, taut leather seat crowned this structure.

Today, the chair is available in both tubular and flat steel. Knoll, the official licensee, calls the models the Tubular Brno Chair and the Flat Bar Brno Chair. Made to the original specifications, the Brno is available in more than 100 fabrics and 500 colours.

☞ **Items to look out for**
If you're buying a 'licensed product' look for the Knoll stamp.

🍷 **Top Tips**
The original version was made from one single piece of stainless steel curved into a C-shape.

Websites
Knoll
www.knoll.com

See also
■ Barcelona Chair, p34

Cité Lounge Chair
Jean Prouvé

One of the most significant designers of the early modern movement, Jean Prouvé produced elegant but functional pieces of furniture, such as the Cité Lounge Chair.

Honoured as one of the most innovative draftsmen and architects of the 20th century, French designer Jean Prouvé became celebrated for his cool, aesthetically pleasing and beautifully constructed designs. The son of artist and sculptor Victor Prouvé who founded the Art Nouveau School of Nancy, Jean Prouvé was apprenticed to an artisan blacksmith at the age of 15 and thus began his long-lasting love of metal. By 1931 he had founded Atelier Jean Prouvé and had begun to make metal furniture. The architect–designer Le Corbusier commented that Prouvé merged the 'soul of an engineer with that of an architect'.

The Cité Lounge Chair (or Arm Chair), which was designed in 1930 for a competition to furnish the halls of residence at Nancy's Cité Universitaire, is an early Prouvé design. Its moulded sheet steel frame, single piece fabric cover, headrest and wide saddle-leather strap armrests make it as current a design today as it was when it was first produced.

☞ **Items to look out for**
The original model is much sought after.

🕯 **Top Tips**
Vitra produces the Cité Lounge Chair from £2,934 (US $4,576).

🌐 **Websites**
Jean Prouvé Museum
www.jeanprouve.com

See also
■ Antony Chair, p104

The Grasshopper
Bruno Mathsson

Acknowledged as one of the most influential Swedish designers and architects of the 20th century, Bruno Mathsson conceived chairs for comfort and aesthetic appeal.

Bruno Mathsson once said that comfortable sitting was viewed as an 'an art' and that it shouldn't be. He made a point of studying the business of sitting to make sure the furniture that he created – such as the 1931 Grasshopper chair – was both functional and beautiful.

As an architect and designer, Mathsson drew on organic forms and the Swedish craft tradition to create objects and buildings that could coexist comfortably with the environment they inhabited. Mathsson designed what was to become known as the Grasshopper chair after he attended the 1930 Stockholm Fair. The Grasshopper was a masterly design, combining a woven webbed seat with a bentwood frame – one arched piece forming the armrest and set of legs. Originally created for the reception area of Värnamo Hospital, the chair was reportedly deemed too ugly to be used by staff there, who gave it the nickname by which it is today known. It was replaced by more traditional seating.

Items to look out for

The original Grasshopper is rare. A limited edition set of 100 was released in 1992 with Mathsson's name stamped on the frame. The outlet Modernity sold a chair recently for £2,500 (US $3,989).

Top Tips

EBay is a good place to look for bargains.

Don't confuse this chair with the Saarinen chair also called The Grasshopper.

Websites
Modernity
www.modernity.se

See also
Eva Chair, p52

41 Paimio
Alvar Aalto

Designed by Alvar Aalto for the comfort of tuberculosis (TB) patients in the Paimio Sanatorium in Finland, the 41 Paimio chair's seamless design has made it popular with collectors.

The 41 Paimio is one of the designs for which Alvar Aalto is most famous. It was created in 1931 for the Paimio Sanatorium, a TB hospital in southwestern Finland for which Aalto designed the building, furniture and fittings. His aim was to design a building and environment that could serve as a 'medical instrument'. Aalto believed that the furnishings and surroundings were as important to a patient's recovery as was his or her treatment. The sanatorium was thus designed to be full of light and had sun terraces where the patients could relax. He also experimented with wood, utilizing its pliant nature to produce a chair that would both be comfortable and through its design help ease a patient's breathing. The frame of the resulting 41 Paimio was made from single pieces of moulded birch plywood bent into closed curves with a single birch cross rail. The seat of the chair was made from one piece of birch plywood. Its flexible structure and angle made the chair very comfortable.

☞ **Items to look out for**
The original 41 Paimio can be found in museums around the world, such as MoMA in New York.

🕯 **Top Tips**
Artek manufactures the 41 Paimio. It can be bought in plywood lacquered in black or white and retails at about £2,570 (US $4,110).

🌐 **Websites**
Artek
www.artek.fi
Skandium
www.skandium.com

See also
■ Model No. 31, p44
　Model No. 60, p46

Model No. 31 (Cantilever Chair)
Alvar Aalto

Since its inception, the cantilever chair has been a favourite with designers. Alvar Aalto's chair is no exception and Model No. 31 is among his most appreciated designs.

Alvar Aalto is one of the most famous Scandinavian designers. His work is diverse, ranging from art glass to buildings and chairs. It is still produced by Artek, the company Aalto co-founded with his wife, Aino Marsio, in 1935. Although Aalto used different materials in his designs, he and Aino experimented with bonding veneers and moulding plywood. It is for his creations using bentwood in the 1930s that he is most celebrated and which led arguably to the creation of one of his most innovative chairs at the time, Model No.31 – the laminated wood cantilever chair. The translation of the steel-tube cantilever frame often used by designers such as Marcel Breuer and Mart Stam into wood made for a more elegant frame. Model No. 31, which was designed for the Paimio Sanatorium, has a plywood seat, back and apron front made from one piece of wood. This is suspended between two U-shaped loops constructed of thick plywood laminate. It is a very beautiful chair.

☞ **Items to look out for**

The original Model No. 31 is still made to Aalto's specifications by Artek.

💡 **Top Tips**

If buying from eBay be careful to check the provenance of the chair.

💻 **Websites**

Artek
www.artek.fi

See also

■ 41 Paimio, p42
Model No. 60, p46

Model No. 60 (Stacking Stool)
Alvar Aalto

Today the stacking stool may seem an obvious concept, but Alvar Aalto's Model No. 60 was groundbreaking at the time of conception. It features in international museum collections.

Alvar Aalto's design philosophy was based on the use of organic materials and natural forms. His reputation as an architect and industrial designer became firmly established after he finished the Paimio Sanatorium in 1932 for which he created two of his most famous chairs, the 41 Paimio and Model No. 31, the cantilever armchair. Aalto's skilful craftsmanship and the lovely fluid lines of his work have influenced many leading designers, including the American couple Charles and Ray Eames.

Originally designed for the Viipuri Library, the Model No. 60 stacking stool was a three-legged bentwood piece with a circular seat. Designed so that several could be easily stacked one on top of the other, Aalto conceived them to save space. When the stools were exhibited in 1933, alongside the 41 Paimio Chair, at London's Fortnum & Mason department store, they caused a sensation. Found in libraries and hospitals around the world, the stool also features in leading design collections.

☞ **Items to look out for**
The original pieces were three-legged bentwood stools.

Top Tips
Artek produce a four-legged version as well as the original design.

Websites
Artek
www.artek.fi

See also
41 Paimio, p42
Model No. 31, p44

Armchair
Gerald Summers

In the 1930s British designer Gerald Summers was also experimenting with bentwood – as were designers such as Alvar Aalto. This 1933–4 armchair is much sought after.

In 1932 British designer Gerald Summers and his wife, Marjorie Amy Butcher, established Makers of Simple Furniture in Britain. It was a relatively small company that mainly produced goods on a made-to-order basis, but it quickly established a reputation for making innovative and beautiful furniture. Summers began to experiment with free-form designs and malleable materials while specializing in using airplane plywood. The armchair, produced in 1933–4, is remarkable in that the arms, seat and feet are created from one piece of wood. Although similar to pieces being produced by Alvar Aalto in Finland, the chair's manufacturing process was different. It involved gluing several thin and pliable veneers together. These were then put into a wooden mould for eight hours, a process that helped create the curvilinear structure that made the chair so appealing. Summers demonstrated the process in a 1938 documentary film. His company closed in 1939.

☞ **Items to look out for**
Only 120 of the original were made.

🔔 **Top Tips**
The original chairs have weak legs that snap easily.

The originals have 'Reg. No. 791116' stamped on a metal plaque that is held by two pins behind the front stretcher.

You can buy a new chair for about £2,197 (US $3,424).

🌐 **Websites**
MoMA
www.moma.org

Zig-Zag Chair
Gerrit Thomas Rietveld

Architect and designer Gerrit Thomas Rietveld was famous for his application of the principles of the De Stijl group. The Zig-Zag Chair and the earlier Red/Blue Chair illustrate this.

The son of an Utrecht cabinetmaker Gerrit Thomas Rietveld learned his craft in his father's workshop at an early age. He worked as a cabinetmaker, running his own shop, while studying architectural drawing. His early work, particularly with wood, gave him the craftsmanship to design and execute his inspirational designs after he joined the De Stijl movement. He first became famous for the Red/Blue Chair, discussed earlier in the book, but it is the cantilevered Zig-Zag Chair that captured the attention of many critics.

A complete departure from other chairs of the time, it had no legs and was sculptural in form. It was also deceptive in that it wasn't made from one piece of wood – as had been the designer's intention – but rather from four, which were metered at the joints apart from where the back met the seat, where it was glued. The pieces were bolted together to give the impression of continuous form.

Cassina now has the licence to produce Gerrit Thomas Rietveld's products.

☞ **Items to look out for**

The original can be found in museum collections around the world.

If you're buying a 'licensed product' look for the engraved signature and certification.

Top Tips

Don't buy the miniature version of the chair – unless you mean to.

Cassina sells a model for about £1,008 (US $1,570) made from cherrywood.

Websites

Cassina
www.cassina.com

See also

■ Red/Blue Chair, p18

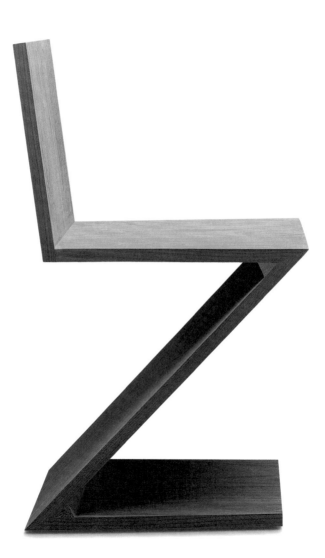

Eva Chair
Bruno Mathsson

Mathsson's 1934 Eva Chair remains one of his most popular designs, even today, more than 70 years after it was first conceived. It built on the success of the earlier Grasshopper.

Found in leading design collections around the world, including New York's prestigious MoMA, Bruno Mathsson's Eva Chair is a modern classic.

A master of Swedish modernism, Mathsson liked to draw on organic shapes and forms and utilize natural materials in his designs, as seen in the early Grasshopper chair. Mathsson came from a family of woodworkers and was trained from an early age in traditional craftsmanship.

The Eva is an easy chair. Produced in 1934, it has clean lines and curves. The originals were made from bent laminated beechwood and woven hemp webbing, but models since then have used different types of wood. Originally manufactured by his father Karl Mathsson's company, which was based in their hometown, Vårnamo, the Eva Chair was praised by critics at the time and quickly became popular with audiences. It is still made today in a range of materials by Bruno Mathsson International. A high-back version is also available.

☞ Items to look out for

The original chair is made from beechwood and bears the Karl Mathsson stamp. Later editions bear the Dux stamp.

🍷 Top Tips

You can pick up a modern Eva Chair for c. £300–500 (US $500–800).

EBay is good for bargains. An original recently sold for £960 (US $1,500).

🌐 Websites

Bruno Mathsson Intl
www.bruno-mathsson-int.com

See also

■ The Grasshopper, p40

Isokon Long Chair
Marcel Breuer

The Isokon Long Chair is one of the earliest examples of biomorphic plywood furniture. It influenced leading designers such as Charles and Ray Eames.

An Isokon sales leaflet, from the 1930s, describes Marcel Breuer's elegant Isokon Long Chair as 'shaped to the human body. It fits you everywhere ... These chairs have all the beauty of right design. Their lines express ease, comfort and well-being.'

Breuer designed the chair shortly after his arrival in England in 1935. Influenced by Bauhaus architect Walter Gropius, who was a consultant for the English company Isokon, Breuer came to work for the firm. Encouraged by Gropius to experiment in plywood and by Isokon owner Jack Pritchard to develop a chair based on his earlier 1932 Aluminium Lounge Chair for a mass-market audience, Breuer came up with the idea of making a chair that would fit or mould to the human form. The subsequent Isokon Long Chair had a bent frame of laminated birch wood, which supported a shaped timber seat and back. While the frames for the prototype were made in London, the bent seats came pre-made from the Venesta Plywood Company in Estonia.

☞ Items to look out for

The original models are rare and hard to get hold of but Isokon Plus makes modern reproductions.

The early models had a mortise and tenon joint.

💡 Top Tips

Modern versions are available in birch, oak or walnut for £1,532 (US $2,450) or with a seat pad in Bute fabric for £2,022 (US $3,235).

🌐 Websites

Isokon Plus
www.isokonplus.com

See also

■ B3, p20
   B32, p28

Pelikan Chair
Finn Juhl

The Scandinavian genius of Finn Juhl is remembered through such designs as the eccentric Pelikan Chair, which debuted at the Cabinetmakers' Guild Exhibition in 1940.

Architect Finn Juhl was one of the leading figures in the Danish design movement of the 1940s. What made Juhl all the more fascinating in a period when many outstanding furniture and industrial designers were emerging from The Royal Danish Academy of Fine Arts, where they were taught by Kaare Klint, was that he was largely self taught. This enabled him to break conventions and challenge accepted forms. In 1937 Juhl made his public debut as a furniture designer at the exhibition of the Copenhagen Cabinetmakers' Guild held at The Royal Danish Academy. His work was quickly acclaimed by audiences. In designs such as the 1940 Pelikan Chair, Juhl produced something very organic but eminently practical as the chair is so comfortable. The original, which was inspired by the designer's interest in modern free art, is rare but very collectable. One Collection manufactures the chair today. It has hand-stitched upholstery and legs made of oak, teak or maple.

Items to look out for

The original 1940 Cabinetmakers' Guild model. One of four known was valued at about £28–32,000 (US $45–50,000).

Top Tips

The Pelikan is available from shops such as Skandium for £4,523 (US $7,900). Its wooden legs come in different types of wood.

Websites

One Collection:
The House of Finn Juhl
www.onecollection.com

Skandium
www.skandium.com

See also

NV-45, p58
Chieftain Chair, p70

NV–45
Finn Juhl

This elegant chair was presented at the Copenhagen Cabinetmakers' Guild Exhibition at the Danish Museum of Art & Design in Copenhagen, 1945.

Finn Juhl was the first Danish furniture designer to be recognized internationally. Like many of his peers, he started off studying architecture but in the late 1930s Juhl began designing furniture primarily for his own use. It was his collaboration with master cabinetmaker Niels Vodder that brought him the most fame. The pair of craftsmen caused a stir at the annual Cabinetmakers' Exhibition of 1945 with designs that were clearly influenced by modern, abstract art.

The NV-45, or Model 45, is one of Juhl's most beautiful pieces of furniture. Conceived in 1945, it broke with the traditional and accepted idea of a chair design by freeing the seat and back from the frame. Upholstered in leather (or fabric), the chair has lovely curved moulded arms and sloping back legs made in high-quality teak showcasing Juhl's attention to detail and his adherence to the use of only the best materials. Today One Collection makes and sells the NV-45.

Items to look out for
The original NV-45 stamped with 'Cabinet Niels Vodder' and 'Design Finn Juhl'.

Top Tips
Original chairs are sold at auction for about £4,250 (US $6,800), but this model can go for as much as £6,875 (US $11,000).

Websites
One Collection:
The House of Finn Juhl
www.onecollection.com
Skandium
www.skandium.com

See also

Pelikan, p56
Chieftain Chair, p70

Moulded Plywood Chairs (LCW/DCW/DCM/LCM)
Charles and Ray Eames

The Eameses created a series of revolutionary moulded plywood chairs – the Lounge Chair Wood (LCW) and Dining Chair Wood (DCW). Versions with metal legs would follow.

In 1945 the LCW and DCW were created as part of a coded range of furniture intended to be affordable to the design-conscious post-war market. Charles Eames worked as a film set designer at the MGM Studio workshops and the original designs for these models used materials that he carefully smuggled out of MGM so that he and Ray could experiment with plywood, glue and rubber. The methods use to mould wood led to the creation of the range of moulded wood furniture for which they became famous. The LCW, the chair that *Time* magazine named 'the best design of the 20th century', is made up of a separate seat and backrest joined by a plywood spine. Its low-slung form hugs the human body and the rubber shock mounts buffer against any jarring movement. The DCM and LCM (Dining Chair Metal and Lounge Chair Metal) are models with metal legs.

Items to look out for
The original 1945–6 plywood model.

Top Tips
Licensed models of the LCW are available from about £485/US $779 to £800/US $1,279.

Check what you buy! Miniature versions are also available.

Look for the official stamp on licensed goods.

Websites
Herman Miller
www.hermanmiller.com
Vitra
www.vitra.com

Womb Chair
Eero Saarinen

When Florence Knoll said that she needed a chair in which she could curl up, designer Eero Saarinen created the Womb Chair and its accompanying Womb Ottoman.

Finnish–American designer and architect Eero Saarinen always pushed the boundaries in terms of design. Saarinen was classically trained in both architecture and sculpture. Both of these disciplines informed his subsequent designs for his interiors and exteriors. The Womb Chair, which was the result of protegée Florence Knoll asking him to create a chair that she could curl up in, showcases the best of Saarinen's design. Providing ultimate comfort to the user, it incorporates the best of contemporary design materials and techniques.

The Womb Chair comprises a steel-rod base with a polished chrome finish and a fibreglass shell frame, which is covered in fabric. The shape of the chair is meant to tempt the user into a relaxed sitting position. Saarinen's aim was to create a chair that would by its design provide emotional comfort and a sense of security by making the user want to curl up in its warmth. Hence, it came to be known as the 'Womb Chair'.

Items to look out for
An official Knoll custom-made Womb Chair and Ottoman can cost up to £2,190 (US $3,500).

Top Tips
Today you can buy the chair in three sizes: small, medium and large (on Knoll website below).

Websites
Knoll
www.knoll.com

See also
■ Tulip Chair, p112

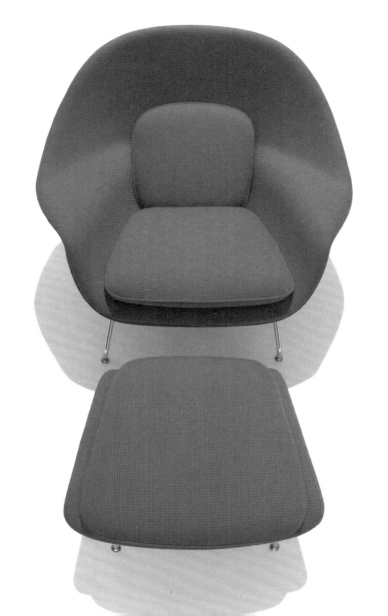

La Chaise
Charles and Ray Eames

The fluid, almost space-age lines of Charles and Ray Eames's La Chaise makes it stand out from their other designs such as the LAR, DAR and RAR.

The evolution of the idea for La Chaise came while Charles and Ray Eames were working with their friend designer and architect Eero Saarinen on plywood chairs for the Organic Design in Home Furnishings Competition held at the Museum of Modern Art (MoMA) in New York in 1947. A year later, La Chaise was born. A startlingly dramatic piece of chair design, the chair's fluid lines were inspired by the sculpture called *Floating Figure* by French artist Gaston Lachaise. The brass sculpture features a woman reclining but seemingly also floating in space; her body is attached to a pedestal. The similarities between the sculpture and La Chaise are quite remarkable. The lines of the chair were made possible by technological advances in moulding fibreglass to create free-form shells for flexible seating. The chair is essentially two fibreglass shells fitted together and painted white. It has a chrome-plated tubular steel frame and a natural solid oak cross-shaped base.

Items to look out for

La Chaise is now produced by Vitra. It can cost about £6,060 (US $9,700).

The early version had a rope or cord edge.

Top Tips

Look for seamless chairs. La Chaise is made to a high-quality specification and is an investment.

Websites

Design Within Reach
www.dwr.com

Vitra: www.vitra.com

See also

■ Moulded Plywood Chairs, p60
LAR, DAR, RAR, p66

■ DSX, DSW, DSR, p84
Model 670 and 671, p116

LAR, DAR and RAR
Charles and Ray Eames

1948-50

LAR, DAR and RAR were a mix-and-match range of chairs that marked the first wave of mass-manufactured plastic chairs.

Beginning in 1948, the Eameses developed a series of interchangeable mix-and-match components that could be made into different chairs. Their aim was to enter the Low Cost Furniture Design Competition held at New York's Museum of Modern Art (MoMA). They made seats, legs and bases of chairs that could be easily assembled or taken apart, using moulded fibreglass seats and metal rod bases. US car manufacturer Chrysler developed welded shock mounts to attach the fibreglass seats to the different bases. The resulting chairs such as the DAR (Dining Armchair Rod) and LAR (Lounge Armchair Rod) had different bases, including the elegant Eiffel Tower-shaped legs, tapering metal-rod legs and the two carved pieces of curved wood that formed rockers for the RAR (Rocker Armchair Rod). Initially available in grey, beige and grey–green, the chairs were manufactured by Herman Miller and Zenith Plastics. The former gave RARs to its employees when they had children.

Items to look out for
Serious collectors look for the Miller–Zenith sticker on the underside.

 Top Tips
Be careful when buying Eames products as there are many fake versions on the market.

 Websites
Herman Miller
www.hermanmiller.com
SCP: www.scp.co.uk
Vitra: www.vitra.com

See also
 Moulded Plywood Chairs, p60
 DSX, DSW, DSR, p84 Model 670 and 671, p116
 Soft Pad Chair, p170

66 – LAR, DAR and RAR

Round Chair (The Chair)
Hans J. Wegner

The Round Chair, also known as 'The Chair', was used in the first televised presidential debate between John F. Kennedy and Richard M. Nixon in 1960.

This elegant chair was created by Danish designer Hans J. Wegner. He believed that furniture should be both functional and beautiful and used natural materials to help make this possible.

Wegner began his career as a cabinetmaker in the early 1930s, but went on to study architecture in Copenhagen, after which he worked in the office of architects Arne Jacobsen and Erik Møller. By the early 1940s, Wegner had set up his own design studio – his attention to detail and excellent craftsmanship quickly won him fans.

The Round Chair, designed in 1949, established his reputation internationally. The chair's clean wood design is pared back to its bare essentials: a semicircle resting on four tapered legs with a cane or leather seat suspended between the legs.

The US magazine *Interiors* called it 'the world's most beautiful chair' and put it on its cover. In 1960, when it was used in the first televised US presidential debate, it achieved cult status.

☞ **Items to look out for**

The original Round Chair is in museums worldwide.

💡 **Top Tips**

Modern versions with leather/woven seats cost £600–700 (US $960–1,120).

🖥 **Websites**

PP Møbler
www.ppdk.com

See also

◻ Wishbone Chair, p72
Folding Chair, p76

◼ Flag Halyard, p82
Teddy Bear Chair, p86
Sawhorse Easy Chair, p94
Cow Horn Chair, p96
Valet Chair, p102

◼ Ox Chair, p140
Shell Chair, p150

Chieftain Chair
Finn Juhl

1949

Inspired by abstract painters and African sculpture, Finn Juhl created the classic Chieftain Chair, which was viewed as quite radical for its time.

Since its inception in the late 1940s, the Chieftain Chair has been produced by various Danish cabinetmakers. Manufactured originally by Niels Vodder in Denmark, the chair received its name when King Frederik IX reportedly sat in the model on display at the 1949 Cabinetmakers' Guild Exhibition in Copenhagen.

Building on some of the principles explored in his earlier NV-45 chair, which separated the sculpturally shaped seat and back from the wooden frame, the Chieftain Chair was inspired by African tribal art and weaponry. The chair's frame is wooden and the seat pads are upholstered in luxurious leather. Its most prominent feature is the armrests, which appear almost sculpted.

During a short period in the 1950s, the US company Baker Furniture acquired the licence to the Chieftain Chair design and produced a limited run. Today, the chair is a much sought-after item.

☞ **Items to look out for**

The original Chieftain Chair is a massive investment, if you can find one. It can retail from £7,190 (US $11,500) upwards

Top Tips

Juhl designed a tray table to go with the chair in 1965.

www **Websites**

One Collection: The House of Finn Juhl
www.onecollection.com

Skandium
www.skandium.com

See also

Pelikan, p56
NV-45, p58

Wishbone Chair
Hans J. Wegner

'The [perfect] chair does not exist,' Wegner commented. 'The good chair is a task one is never completely done with.' The Wishbone is, for many critics, almost perfect.

Hans J. Wegner trained to be a cabinetmaker, before he studied at the Copenhagen School of Art and Crafts. His chairs were made as stand-alone pieces and are beautiful objects in their own right. The designer believed that 'stripping the old chairs of their outer style and letting them appear in their pure construction' helped achieve this aim.

The Wishbone Chair (or 'Y Chair'), which Wegner produced for Carl Hansen and Son, was part of his Chinese Chair Series. Influenced by portraits of Danish merchants sitting on Ming chairs, the Wishbone mixes the old with the new – the steam-bending of timber and the weaving of cord seats with an original modern twist.

Wegner collaborated on many of his designs with Johannes Hansen, a master cabinetmaker. Both men loved working with wood. It was certainly Wegner's material of choice when designing and something he deemed essential for making the perfect chair.

Items to look out for

Available in a range of timbers and colours. £445 to £550 (US $710–880).

Top Tips

An original's top rail is one piece of steam-bent wood. Copies have two joins.

The older versions have a burned stamp not a sticker.

Websites

Carl Hansen and Son
www.carlhansen.com

See also

Round Chair, p68
Folding Chair, p76

Flag Halyard, p82
Teddy Bear Chair, p86
Sawhorse Easy Chair, p94

Shell Chair, p150

The Colonial Chair (PJ 149)
Ole Wanscher

Ole Wanscher's beautiful designs were inspired by a wide range of sources – from Egyptian and Greek furniture to English period design. The Colonial Chair is a classic.

Danish designer Ole Wanscher studied under Kaare Klint and was professor of the Furniture School at the Royal Academy in Copenhagen. He believed in producing beautiful furniture for a mass-market audience at affordable prices. He was influenced by many different styles of design, as his work shows, and among his most famous and popular pieces is the 1949 Colonial Chair (PJ 149), which is still very sought after today.

Made of rosewood and leather, the PJ 149 had cane seats that wrapped around the inside of the seat frame. It was an elegantly constructed chair that combined comfort with style. Manufactured by P. Jeppesens Møbelfabrik A/S (today PJ Furniture A/S), the originals bear the maker's mark. On the centenary of Wanscher's death PJ Furniture produced three of his designs, including 150 limited editions of the Colonial Chair. The chairs are upholstered in vegetable leather in Indian red, black and natural.

☞ **Items to look out for**

You can pick up the **Colonial Chair** at auction for about £4,000 (US $6,233).

The limited edition – 150 chairs produced in 2003 to mark the centenary of the designer's birth.

💡 **Top Tips**

There are modern versions of the chair available in mahogany, American cherry, walnut, maple, oak and ash with a wide range of cushion designs, in fabric or oxhide.

🖳 **Websites**

PJ Furniture A/S
www.pj-furniture.com

Folding Chair (JH 512)
Hans J. Wegner

Largely responsible for making Danish design a byword on modern collectors' lips, Hans J. Wegner produced a huge number of chairs, including the elegant JH 512.

During his long career, the iconic Danish designer Hans J. Wegner created more than 500 chairs, many of which feature in this book. For Wegner, a chair was not just a functional object but also a piece of art, meant to be aesthetically pleasing. Many pieces, such as the Valet Chair, not only reveal his quirky sense of humour but also illustrate how the designer often created goods to fulfil his own needs as a consumer.

In 1949, Wegner designed the JH 512, a folding chair made of solid oak and cane. Wegner's aim was to make an armchair that could be stowed away easily.

The design that Wegner eventually created was striking in its simplicity and was a brilliant solution to the problem of how to store such a chair – he designed the piece so that it could be folded up and hung on a wall.

Originally manufactured by Johannes Hansen Møbelsnedkeri A/S, the Folding Chair was later produced from 1991 onwards by PP Møbler.

Items to look out for

A pair of original 1949 chairs made of oak, cane, brass with 'Johannes Hansen /Copenhagen/Denmark' and the manufacturer's mark stamped on the frame can reach about £6–7,000 (US $10–12,000).

Top Tips

PP Møbler makes the chair in different woods.

Websites

PP Møbler
www.pp.dk

See also

Round Chair, p68
Wishbone Chair, p72

Flag Halyard, p82
Teddy Bear Chair, p86
Sawhorse Easy Chair, p94

Ax Chair
Hvidt and Mølgaard-Nielsen

The first Danish chair to have a seat and back designed from double-curved laminated wood, the Ax Chair quickly became popular with design-conscious consumers.

Inspired by the furniture and methods of Charles and Ray Eames in the United States, the Ax Chair was first produced by Fritz Hansen in Denmark. It was unusual for the time in that it was made from double-curved laminated wood using a glueing process that Fritz Hansen had borrowed from the manufacturing process for tennis rackets. The fact that the back and seat were easily dismantled meant that the chair could essentially be taken apart for easy shipping abroad.

Both the Ax Chair and an accompanying table were displayed at the 1951 Good Show at MoMA in New York. The pieces established the reputation of their designers, architects Peter Hvidt and Orla Mølgaard-Nielsen, who had first begun working together in 1944. Over the next decades the pair would design more than 250 objects, many considered iconic and collectable. Today, the Ax Chair is available in various woods, with a leather or upholstered seat option, with and without arms.

☞ **Items to look out for**
The original Ax Chairs have the Fritz Hansen stamp on. They can be found for about £455 (US $708).

🛈 **Top Tips**
Some of the older versions also have upholstery. The chair held in the V&A collection in London, owned by Isokon founder Jack Pritchard in 1950, has a detachable fabric seat.

An accompanying Ax Table is available.

🖵 **Websites**
Retro Modern Design
www.retromoderndesign.com

Hunting Chair
Børge Mogensen

Most of Danish designer Børge Mogensen's products combine functionality with clean and strong lines – the 1950 Hunting Chair showcases this .

Børge Mogensen benefited greatly from the influence of his mentor Kaare Klint. Mogensen spent many years at the Copenhagen School of Arts and Crafts and also worked as Klint's teaching assistant at the Royal Academy.

In 1950 Mogensen designed what was to become known as the Hunting Chair for the interior of a hunting lodge at the autumn exhibition of the Copenhagen Cabinetmakers' Guild. The chair design used techniques that Mogensen was to fine-tune and use in later models such as the Spanish Chair (1959).

Made of a solid oak frame with a stretched leather back and seat, this low easy chair was very cleanly and solidly constructed. In that same year, it was manufactured by Erhard Rasmussen. The chair was also imported to Britain by Finmar Ltd and shown at an exhibition at the National Portrait Gallery in London in 1962. Today it is made in Denmark by Fredericia Furniture.

☞ **Items to look out for**
The original chair was manufactured by Erhard Rasmussen and bears its stamp.

💡 **Top Tips**
Fredericia Furniture is the licensed producer of this chair, which costs about £3,147 (US $4,899).

🌐 **Websites**
Danish Design Store
www.danishdesignstore.com

See also
■ Spanish Chair, p138

Flag Halyard (PP 205)
Hans J. Wegner

The Flag Halyard chair is unique because it breaks with the tradition of Wegner's previous chair designs but is still quintessentially a Wegner design.

The Flag Halyard chair, so the story goes, was conceived by Hans J Wegner while he was on a beach during a family holiday in Arhus. He is alleged to have spent a lot of time drawing and redrawing the shape of the seat in the sand. Whether this is true, without a doubt, the Flag Halyard is a unique chair, one that is different from Wegner's predominantly wood-based chairs.

The chair, which Wegner designed in about 1950, pays more than a nod to modernists such as Marcel Breuer and Mies van der Rohe in its use of chrome-plated steel pipes in the frame. This industrial look is softened by the use of plaited Flag Halyard and sheepskin. The armrest, seat and back are made from one 240-metre (262-yard) long unbroken piece of flag halyard.

In 2002, the company PP Møbler won the Bo Bedre's Classics Award when it began to manufacture the chair again. It is the licensed producer.

☞ **Items to look out for**
The original chair is very collectable.

🍷 **Top Tips**
A version by PP Møbler made to the original specifications costs about £8,487(US $13,225).

🌐 **Websites**
PP Møbler
www.ppdk.com

See also

DSX, DSW and DSR
Charles and Ray Eames

Husband-and-wife team Charles and Ray Eames continued to experiment with industrial materials during the 1940s and '50s. Their range of low-cost plastic side chairs was the result.

Charles and Ray Eames wanted to produce high-quality beautifully designed affordable goods for mass-market consumers. The DSX (Dining Height Side Chair X-Base opposite), DSW (Dining Height Side Chair Wood) and DSR (Dining Height Side Chair with Rod Base), their plastic side-chair series, is a modern take on their classic fibreglass chairs.

The DSX has a polypropylene seat shell, dyed through and a chrome or powder coated base with four legs. Like the LAR, DAR and RAR, the Dining Height Side Chair Series features the same shell bases but has different bases. It was created in association with Zenith Plastics for the Low Cost Furniture Design Competition at MoMA. These plastic side chairs were very successful.

The Eameses also created the popular DKW-2 (Dining Height K [Wire Seat] Wood Legs [-2]) in 1951. Made of black metal wire and birch legs, it had what Herman Miller termed a 'two piece' brown leather pad, but the public called the 'Bikini Pad'.

☞ **Items to look out for**

The original chairs have the Zenith Plastics stamp.

💡 **Top Tips**

It is possible to pick up a licensed chair for just over £179 (US $232) at Heal's.

Websites

Vitra
www.vitra.com

Herman Miller
www.hermanmiller.com

See also

▪ Moulded Plywood Chairs, p60
▪ DSX, p84
  Model 670 and 671, p116
▪ Soft Pad Chair, p170

Teddy Bear Chair (PP19)
Hans J. Wegner

The PP19, also known as the Teddy Bear Chair or PaPa Bear Chair, is one of Hans J. Wegner's most popular and also most desired chairs.

Manufactured in the early 1950s, the PP19 was created both as a work of art and also essentially to support the human form. Like Wegner's other work, this lovely chair places comfort and functionality alongside beauty and craftsmanship. The PP19 is both playful and organic in design. The chair received its name after a critic referred to its armrests as 'great bear paws embracing you from behind'. It is best known as the Teddy Bear Chair today and sums up the designer's belief that a chair should be beautiful from all sides and angles. Wegner also designed a footstool, known as the PP120, for the chair.

Originally manufactured by AP Stolen, the chair frames were supplied by the PP Møbler workshop, which would go on to produce Wegner designs in the late 1960s. The production of the chair resumed in 2003 to commemorate PP Møbler's 50th anniversary. Some people also refer to it as the PaPa Bear Chair.

☞ **Items to look out for**
The Teddy Bear Chair costs from £5,000 (US $8,000).

💡 **Top Tips**
Also called the PaPa Bear Chair.

The PP120 is the footstool designed for the PP19.

🌐 **Websites**
Danish Design Store
www.danishdesignstore.com
PP Møbler
www.ppdk.com

See also

▉ Round Chair, p68
Folding Chair, p76

▉ Sawhorse Easy Chair, p94
Cow Horn Chair, p96
Valet Chair, p102

Antelope Chair
Ernest Race

In the 1951 Festival of Britain, in which the best of the nation's design was showcased, visitors could sit on Ernest Race's now-classic Antelope Chair (and Bench) in the exhibition grounds.

In the years following the end of the Second World War, there was a great spirit of optimism. In Britain and the United States, a new generation of designers were experimenting with the innovative materials developed during the war but many still possessed the frugal and rational mentality of the war years. In 1951 the Festival of Britain, held on the centenary of the Great Exhibition, opened on London's remodelled South Bank to celebrate and promote British industry and design.

On the exhibition terraces visitors could sit on Ernest Race's almost whimsical lightweight Antelope Chair (and Bench). The curved chair frame was made of fine bent steel rods and at the end of each of its splayed spindly four legs were almost comic metal balls, which were meant to call to mind nuclear physics and molecular chemistry. The moulded plywood seat was painted in the Festival colours of red, grey, yellow or blue. It was designed to sum up the spirit of optimism in Britain.

☞ **Items to look out for**
The original chair is featured in museums worldwide.

💡 **Top Tips**
A modern version of the chair costs about £500 (US $860).

🖥 **Websites**
Race Furniture www.racefurniture.com

Lady Chair
Marco Zanuso

Marco Zanuso's sensuously curved, rubber-foam upholstered chair won the gold medal at the Milan Triennale in 1951. Visually exciting, it raised industrial standards at the time.

Italian-born Marco Zanuso is one of the fathers of modernism. Like many important designers of the 20th century, he was trained in architecture and from 1945 to 1986 was Professor of Architecture, Design and Town Planning at the Polytechnic of Milan. He was also involved in setting up the Triennale exhibitions in Milan.

In the 1940s he began to experiment in bent metal. The Lady Chair was designed fairly early in his career and came about as a result of the tyre manufacturer Pirelli, which asked him to design seating utilizing foam rubber. Pirelli established a new division, Arflex, to manufacture such a product. Zanuso's 1951 Lady Chair is a subtly curved and elegant piece. Based on a timber frame the chair has a fabric-covered rubber-foam upholstery. The main body of the chair sits on tubular chrome metal legs. Zanuso designed the chair in 1951 and it was awarded the gold medal at the prestigious Milan Triennale.

☞ **Items to look out for**
The original chair sells for about £3,209 (US $5,000) and was manufactured by Arflex. A label appears on the chair's underside.

🔖 **Top Tips**
More modern versions are available in different colours.

〰️ **Websites**
Design within reach
www.dwr.com

Ant (Model 3100)
Arne Jacobsen

The Ant chair was produced by Arne Jacobsen in the 1950s. He could see the exciting possibilities of combining plywood, tubular metal and new industrial techniques in chair design.

The Ant, or Model 3100, was the predecessor of the Series 7 chair, also featured in this book. First produced in the early 1950s by Danish master Arne Jacobsen, it was, in many ways, a product of its time. The post-war years had seen designers take advantage of the new techniques and materials that had become available in the 1930s and 40s, often through the work of such people as Charles and Ray Eames. Jacobsen saw the possibilities of using materials that had been popular in the past – plywood and tubular metal – with new industrial techniques in mass-produced furniture. Plywood was not only very malleable, but it was also cheap, light and could be easily laminated or coloured. Jacobsen began to experiment and came up with the Ant, a chair with a back and seat made of one piece of intricately moulded plywood – and rather shockingly for the time had no arms. It also had only three legs. It was originally produced for the canteen at Novo Nordic, a Danish healthcare company, but since then it has sold in its millions.

☞ **Items to look out for**

The 1951–2 chair is made of one piece of moulded plywood and three steel legs.

Top Tips

Modern chairs come with three and four (stackable) legs in a range of colours. Fritz Hansen makes them. A three-legged version sells for about £350 (US $545).

Websites

Fritz Hansen
www.fritzhansen.com

See also

■ Model 3107, p110
  Egg Chair, p122
  Swan Chair, p126
  Drop Chair, p136

Sawhorse Easy Chair (CH28)
Hans J. Wegner

By 1952, Hans J. Wegner had already established a reputation for beautifully crafted furniture. The Sawhorse Easy Chair (CH28) added to this esteem.

Pretty much every design collection in the world possesses an item – usually a chair – designed by Hans J. Wegner. The Danish architect began his career working with design legend Arne Jacobsen in Århus in 1940, also the year that he began his long-standing extremely profitable collaboration with master cabinetmaker Johannes Hansen, who produced many of Wegner's chairs.

In 1952 Wegner decided to design an easy chair made of wood. Although the designer worked in different materials, his training and skill as a cabinetmaker made him most comfortable when working with wood. The CH28 illustrates Wegner's great skill. Originally made of oak and teak, the CH28 or Sawhorse (also known as the Sawback) Easy Chair was one of the first five designs that Wegner made for Carl Hansen and Son. Its beauty lies in its construction, which relies heavily on the relationship between the joining of the rear post, the front leg and the arm.

☞ **Items to look out for**
The original 1952 chair was produced in oak/teak.

♟ **Top Tips**
The Sawhorse costs about £1,996 (US $3,108) for a pure oak chair and £2,019 (US $3,145) for an oak/walnut chair.

www **Websites**
Carl Hansen
www.carlhansen.com

See also
■ Round Chair, p68
   Folding Chair, p76
■ Teddy Bear Chair, p86
   Sawhorse Easy Chair, p94
   Cow Horn Chair, p96
   Valet Chair, p102
■ Shell Chair, p150

Cow Horn Chair (PP 505)
Hans J. Wegner

Prolific designer Hans J. Wegner produced some of his most iconic work in the 1950s. The Cow Horn Chair can be seen in many international design museums.

In 1952 Hans J. Wegner designed what was to become known as the Cow Horn Chair (Kohom Stolen). To some critics it is reminiscent of a Juhl chair, its curving back and top rail leading to this comparison. For others it is typically Wegner, beautifully crafted in wood, with clean and fluid lines and simple shapes – as seen in the Round Chair.

Made for Johannes Hansen's studio, the chair was so-named because of the shape of its top rail and back, which were reminiscent of a cow's horns. It was originally made of teak and rosewood with a cane seat. It was conceived to be functional and the curved top rail means that the chair can be easily drawn in at a table and the cane seat and curved back allow for maximum comfort. These chairs are very collectable – in 2009, at a Sotheby's auction of 20th-century design, 10 Hans J. Wegner Cow Horn Chairs were sold for US $65,500 (£41,000), a record price for this classic chair. In 1991 PP Møbler resumed production of the chair.

☞ **Items to look out for**

The original in MoMA.

Top Tips

It can also be bought today with a leather or fabric seat for about £249 (US $389).

Websites

PP Møbler
www.ppdk.com

See also

■ Round Chair, p68
  Folding Chair, p76
■ Teddy Bear Chair, p86
  Sawhorse Easy Chair, p94
  Valet Chair, p102
■ Shell Chair, p150

Bird Chair and Ottoman
Harry Bertoia

Harry Bertoia's sculptural chairs for Knoll were groundbreaking for their time. Even today the classic shape and design of the Bird Chair and Ottoman fascinate collectors.

Born Arieto Bertoia in 1915, his name was anglicized to 'Harry' when he moved to the United States at the age of 15. A talented artist, by 1937 he was attending Cranbrook Academy of Art and was taught by some of the most talented artists and designers of the time, including Walter Gropius. Fellow students included Charles and Ray Eames and Florence Schust (the future Mrs Knoll). This group of people were very important to his later career.

After experimenting in plywood with the Eameses, Bertoia became interested in body dynamics. Florence and Hans Knoll invited him to work with them in Pennsylvania, giving him free reign to design whatever he wanted with full credit. He produced the Bird Chair and Ottoman in 1952, having developed a metal-wire grid that could be bent at will making it flexible and suited to a body's contours. Bertoia believed that chairs should be adaptable and that sitting in one should be like wearing a 'comfortable coat'.

☞ **Items to look out for**
The original chair and ottoman from 1952.

🕯 **Top Tips**
Stil manufactured by Knoll, the Bird is available in different fabrics.

www **Websites**
Knoll
www.knoll. com

See also
■ Diamond Chair, p100

Diamond Chair
Harry Bertoia

An instantly recognizable chair, the lightweight and beautifully constructed Diamond Chair is probably one of Harry Bertoia's most popular designs.

Italian-born Harry Bertoia was a sculptor and furniture designer. He designed the now-famous metalwork Diamond Chair for Knoll in the 1950s and the chair won the Designer of the Year award in 1955. It was a financial success despite having to be handcrafted. The income enabled Bertoia to concentrate on his true love, sculpture.

Bertoia had worked with Charles and Ray Eames in the 1940s. He contributed to the development of the classic LCW (Lounge Chair Wood), before he set up his own studio in Pennsylvania in 1950.

The Diamond Chair was designed to appear different from every angle. Produced almost entirely from wire mesh, the light frame was created from steel rods and its design reflects Bertoia's training as a sculptor. He commented that the chairs were largely made of air, just like light sculptures, saying: 'I wanted my chair to rotate, change with movement' and to this end he was very successful. Knoll manufacture the chair today.

☞ **Items to look out for**
An official Knoll custom-made large Diamond Chair retails from £1,335 (US $2,085).

💡 **Top Tips**
Today a child's version is also available from Knoll for about £353 (US $550).

🌐 **Websites**
Knoll
www.knoll.com

See also
■ Bird Chair and Ottoman, p98

Valet Chair (PP250)
Hans J. Wegner

1953

Fashion designer Karl Lagerfeld reportedly asked his parents for a Valet Chair. Whether that's true or not, the chair is a masterly design, combining simplicity, form and function.

Among Hans J. Wegner's most admired designs, the Valet Chair was created to help hang or store a man's suit. In much of the designer's work, the quixotic blends with the practical; the fun with the sublime. The PP250, or Valet Chair, is an example of this. Reportedly conceived after Wegner had a discussion with architecture professor Steen Eiler Rasmussen and designer Bo Bojesen about the best method to fold clothes at night-time, the Valet Chair is both functional and sculptural in form. The top rail is shaped as a coat hanger while the seat flips up to hang trousers. The seat also covers a box for the storage of items such as keys, a wallet or cards – the kind of items one might store in suit pockets. The original prototype had four legs, but Wegner was dissatisfied with the look, deeming it too heavy. He continued working on the design and ended up removing one of the legs. The chair was originally made of teak and solid pine with leather and brass details.

☞ Items to look out for
The original model was made of solid pine with an oiled teak seat. In 2010 at auction one sold for over £13,125 (US $21,000).

🕯 Top Tips
More modern reproductions are available, some in ash.

PP Møbler's modern version doesn't come cheap at about £4,500 (US $7,200).

🖥 Websites
PP Møbler
www.ppdk.com

See also
■ Folding Chair, p76
■ Teddy Bear Chair, p86
  Sawhorse Easy Chair, p94
  Cow Horn Chair, p96
■ Shell Chair, p150

Antony Chair (Model 356)
Jean Prouvé

The Antony Chair was one of Jean Prouvé's last designs. The elegant lines of the exposed painted bent tubular and flat steel frame and moulded plywood seat are beautiful.

Influential designer Jean Prouvé was once quoted as saying 'never design anything that cannot be made'. Prouvé, who trained in engineering, was interested in merging the best of manufacturing techniques with beautiful design and it is this combination that has not only given his products longevity, but has also inspired designers and architects such as Norman Foster and Renzo Piano in their work. At his factory near Nancy in north-east France, Prouvé designed, conducted research and development and produced many of his best works, although he lost control of it in 1953.

For many people, the Antony Chair, produced in 1954, is one of his greatest designs. Based on an earlier work, produced in 1950 for the University of Strasbourg, Prouvé designed the elegant Antony for the student rooms at the Maison de la Tunisie and Maison du Mexique at the Cité Universitaire. He worked on the commission with the acclaimed architect and designer Charlotte Perriand.

☞ **Items to look out for**
The original chair.

💡 **Top Tips**
The chair sells for as little as £678 (US $1,048).

Be careful not to buy one of the accurate miniatures produced by Vitra for about £149 (US $269).

🖥 **Websites**
Heals
www.heals.com

See also
■ Cité Lounge Chair, p38

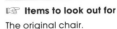

Butterfly Stool
Sori Yanagi

Sori Yanagi worked with influential French designer Charlotte Perriand in her Tokyo-based practice. After setting up an industrial design institute, Yanagi designed the Butterfly Stool.

In 1954, Sori Yanagi designed the Butterfly Stool. It consists of two molded plywood elements held together essentially by a metal rod. The Butterfly Stool is so called because of its graceful curvilinear form, which is also reminiscent of a fleetingly jotted-down script character in Japanese calligraphy. In creating it, Yanagi used the same plywood-moulding techniques that husband-and-wife team Charles and Ray Eames invented in the 1950s to produce their mass-market furniture designs. Yanagi put together two identical moulded-plywood forms, which were held together by a simple brass stretcher. Originally made by Tendo Co., the Butterfly meshed eastern and western aesthetics. Today, the stool is produced by Vitra and has a maple or palisander veneer. An optional seat cushion in red Hallingdal upholstery fabric is also available.

The Butterfly Stool can be found in leading museum collections around the world.

☞ **Items to look out for**
The **Butterfly Stool** retails from £400 (US $645) at Vitra-approved sellers. At auction, be prepared to pay several thousand pounds for an original.

Top Tips
The **Butterfly Stool** can be found on auction sites but check the provenance of the item for sale carefully.

Websites
Vitra
www.vitra.com

Coconut Chair
George Nelson

George Nelson took his inspiration for this classic 1955 chair from the cracked section of a coconut. It is one of his most recognizable chairs.

George Nelson said: 'No design can exist in isolation. It is always related, sometimes in very complex ways, to an entire constellation of influencing situations and attitudes.' Nelson's own many fabulous designs took their inspiration from a variety of sources.

The Coconut Chair, designed by Nelson in 1955, and produced by Herman Miller, the company for which he was director of design, is inspired by a coconut – as Nelson commented it was based on one piece of a coconut that had been cut up into eight sections. In creating it Nelson wanted to produce a seat that was stylish, comfortable and that would suit a person no matter what position he or she assumed. Despite the Coconut Chair having a very light appearance it is quite a heavy product due to the shell, which is made of steel. This is upholstered in a fabric-covered foam and sits on top of three tubular steel and metal rod legs, which give the chair its contemporary look.

☞ **Items to look out for**

Herman Miller still sells the Coconut for about £2,887 (US $4,499).

🍴 **Top Tips**

You can buy a high-quality reproduction 'inspired' Coconut Chair for as little as £379 (US $579).

www **Websites**

Herman Miller
www. hermanmiller.com

See also

■ MAA, p130

Model 3107 (Series 7)
Arne Jacobsen

Since its creation, Model 3107, the Series 7 chair, has sold more than five million copies around the world. The 1963 photo of Christine Keeler straddling it arguably helped increase sales.

Influenced by the idea that every element was important in the creation of truly good design – from the 'spoon to the city' – Arne Jacobsen strived to create perfection in every object or space that he designed. In the 1950s, his eyes increasingly turned towards industrial product design. He was particularly interested in the work and methods of Charles and Ray Eames.

The 3100 chair, produced in the mid 1950s was made of a moulded-plywood frame set on three rather spindly-looking steel legs and became known as the 'Ant'. That chair was arguably essential to the evolution of Model 3107, the design for which Jacobsen is probably best known to popular audiences.

A compact, light hourglass-shaped plywood body on four steel legs, Model 3107 was extremely comfortable to sit on. It was also attractive when viewed from any angle. The chair soon became a runaway success.

☞ **Items to look out for**

The original Series 7 chairs were hand produced.

In 2005, Fritz Hansen made a children's version, at three-quarters of the original size.

🍸 **Top Tips**

Look for the Fritz Hansen mark.

This is the most copied chair. If you pay £10 (US $16) it is most likely to be a fake.

The original chair has a 3D curve and no straight edges.

🌐 **Websites**

Design Within Reach
www.dwr.com

Fritz Hansen
www.fritzhansen.com

Tulip (Model 150)
Eero Saarinen

Eero Saarinen believed in creating fluid, organic-looking furniture by using modern manufacturing techniques and materials. The Tulip Chair is an example of his approach.

Probably one of the most recognizable of Eero Saarinen's many designs, the Tulip Chair has reached iconic status not just for its futuristic design but also because it was used in the cult US television series *Star Trek* between 1966 and 1969.

Part of the last series of furniture that Saarinen designed, the Tulip is so named after the flower its lines so clearly resemble. Other critics have compared it to a wine glass. Either way, the Tulip Chair was the culmination of Saarinen's design concept of creating one piece from one material. Certainly it looks as if that is the case. In reality, the chair is made of fibreglass, aluminium and plastic. The shell seat is sculpted fibreglass and the stem has a fused-plastic finish that covers the aluminium stem supporting the tulip-head seat. Saarinen wanted to create a clean, classic, uncluttered piece – a chair with a single leg instead of the mess of legs that created 'an ugly, confusing, unrestful world' in modern interiors, according to the designer.

☞ **Items to look out for**

The Tulip Chair dating from 1955–6.

The 50th Anniversary Collection produced by Knoll, which came with a commemorative medal and a certificate of authentication.

🍸 **Top Tips**

You can buy the chair today with arms for £905 (US $1,446) and without arms for £825 (US $1,323).

If you're buying a licensed product, look for the Knoll stamp.

www **Websites**

Knoll: www.knoll.com

See also

▧ Womb Chair, p62

PK22
Poul Kjærholm

Poul Kjærholm based the steel frame structure of the PK22 on that of the 'Element Chair', the design from his graduation project at the School of Applied Arts in Copenhagen.

Born in 1929 in Denmark, Poul Kjærholm trained as a carpenter before joining the Danish School of Arts and Crafts. He worked at Fritz Hansen for a year where he produced some of his finest works. Fritz Hansen still produces the PK22 Chair, one of the 1950s' designs for which Kjærholm is best known.

Kjærholm liked to use organic materials, including steel, which he rated as a natural product. His elegant, pared-down designs are immediately recognizable for their almost sculptural clean, simple lines. The PK22, produced in 1955–6, is an example of this kind of design. Made of a classic thin canvas (leather or woven cane) back and seat, which sat on a flattened chrome-plated steel frame, the chair won the Grand Prix at the Milan Triennale in 1957. It was an immediate commercial success.

From 1955 until his death in 1980, Kjærholm collaborated with manufacturer Ejvind Kold Christensen. In 1982 Fritz Hansen took over the production and sales of 'The Kjærholm Collection'.

☞ **Items to look out for**
The PK22 can cost from £3,430 (US $5,344).

🍴 **Top Tips**
The reissued chair is available in the original canvas and colours: umber green, primary red and black.

🌐 **Websites**
Fritz Hansen
www.fritzhansen.com

Model 670 and Model 671 (Lounge Chair and Ottoman) Charles and Ray Eames

Created as a gift for the movie director Billy Wilder, the Lounge Chair and Ottoman were a departure from the mass-manufactured products previously created by the Eameses.

Today a highly sought-after collector's item, the Lounge Chair and its accompanying Ottoman were Charles and Ray Eames's take on the English classic club chair and footstool. Charles Eames said that he wanted to create a chair with the 'warm, receptive look of a well-used first baseman's mitt'. In the chair's squashed but sumptuous leather upholstery that makes anyone viewing it want to immediately sink down into its comfort, the Model 670 meets that end. The Eameses launched their Lounge Chair and Ottoman during an interview in 1956 with Arlene Francis for the NBC programme *Home*. In a very clever and slightly irreverent short movie set to music, the chair and ottoman are seen being easily constructed from the base upwards, enjoyed by the man who had put them together and then deconstructed, only to end up back in a well-designed Herman Miller box.

☞ Items to look out for

The original model with a shell made from Brazilian rosewood.

♟ Top Tips

Still hand assembled, the shells are seven-ply cherry, natural cherry, walnut, or santos palisander. Together, the chair and ottoman cost £4,777 (US $7,640).

There are a plethora of cheap, low-quality copies, particularly from China.

🖳 Websites

Herman Miller
www.hermanmiller.com
The Conran Shop
www.conranshop.co.uk
Vitra: www.vitra.com

Superleggera 699
Gio Ponti

Italian master Gio Ponti is a leading light in terms of 20th-century design. The Superleggera, the chair he designed in 1957, is probably his most recognized work.

Gio Ponti was a master of many trades – architect, designer, illustrator, poet and critic.

Born in Milan in 1891, Ponti began to study architecture only to have his studies in interrupted by the outbreak of the First World War. Although he finished his degree, his first major job was working as the art director of Richard–Ginori, the ceramics manufacturer. In the seven years he worked there he transformed the company into a cutting-edge ceramics firm.

In 1928, Ponti set up the magazine *Domus* to promote his ideas and beliefs. At the end of the 1920s he started to design buildings including one housing the Maths Department at Rome University. Over the decades he worked in other areas, including costume and industrial design. The 1957 Superleggera pays a nod to the Chiavari chairs found on the beaches of the Italian Riviera. Using modern materials, Ponti created a light, classic chair that could be made cheaply and easily.

☞ **Items to look out for**
The Superleggera can cost about £1,068 (US $1,665).

🎯 **Top Tips**
The original Superleggera is so light that a child can pick it up with one finger.

🌐 **Websites**
Cassina
www.cassina.com

Mezzadro
Achille and Pier
Giacomo Castiglioni

Achille and Pier Giacomo Castiglioni are responsible for some of the most stunning 20th-century designs. The fascinating Mezzadro stool and Sella Chair are among them.

Considered to be one of Achille and Pier Giacomo Castiglioni's more radical designs, the Mezzadro stool was only put into production by Zanotta in the 1980s.

Paying more than a nod to Surrealism, the stool, some critics comment, is the design equivalent of French artist Marcel Duchamp's 'Readymades', art made from manufactured bits and pieces, such as the 1913 Bicycle Wheel, which featured a wheel mounted onto a stool. The Castiglionis' Mezzadro is constructed from a seat and crossbar taken from an old Italian tractor. The lacquered seat is balanced on a chrome-plated steel stem.

Today, the seat comes in a variety of colours: aluminium, orange, red, yellow, white or black – and the footrest is made of natural steam-treated beech. The Sella Chair, with its black racing-bike saddle seat atop a pink steel column, was part of the same series as the Mezzadro.

☞ **Items to look out for**

The original Mezzadro.

The 50 numbered and signed special-edition chairs produced in different colours for the Mezzadro's 50th anniversary by Zanotta.

♟ **Top Tips**

A modern Zanotta-produced Mezzadro sells for about £582 (US $906).

Don't buy the miniature by mistake. Check the dimensions carefully.

🖳 **Websites**

Unica Home www.unicahome.com

Egg Chair
Arne Jacobsen

Jacobsen was a prolific and influential designer, producing everything from beautiful lighting and cutlery to his famous chairs, such as the classic Egg Chair.

Originally created in the 1950s for the SAS Royal Hotel in Copenhagen, the Egg Chair is instantly recognizable and much knocked off in terms of faux versions (see Top Tips right).

Jacobsen's unique take on the traditional winged chair, the Egg Chair features a 360-degree swivel base. The seat is composed of upholstered foam and fibreglass. The base consists of a satin-polished, welded steel tube attached to an injection-moulded aluminium cross. Originally intended for the lobby and reception areas of SAS Royal Hotel, the Egg Chair began its life as a plaster cast in Jacobsen's garage. The chair provides the user with a certain amount of privacy, the wings screening him or her from view. Jacobsen designed it with a matching ottoman – on a similar steel and aluminium base – and the chair can be bought with or without it. In 2008 for the 50th anniversary of the Egg Chair, Fritz Hansen invited Israeli artist Tal R to cover 50 of Jacobsen's chairs.

☞ **Items to look out for**

The original Fritz Hansen model sells for upwards of £3,750 (US $6,000). It is 110cm (43in) high, with taut fabric and a top-stitched single seam.

🍷 **Top Tips**

There are several far cheaper but credible copies on the market for less than a quarter of the official price. Restoration Hardware, for example, sells the Copenhagen Chair, which is 5cm (2in) higher than the original and has double roll-and-tuck seams.

🌐 **Websites**

Fritz Hansen
www.fritzhansen.com

Hive Modern
www.hivemodern.com

Egg
Nanna Ditzel

Danish designer Nanna Ditzel's love of nature and interest
in new techniques allowed her to create works such as
the iconic hanging Egg.

Born in Copenhagen in 1923, Nanna Ditzel trained as
a cabinetmaker before attending the School of Arts
and Crafts and the Royal Academy of Fine Arts in the
city. She set up a studio with her husband Jørgen Ditzel
after graduating in furniture design.

In the post-war years, Ditzel became well known
for her experimentation with new techniques and
materials. She incorporated fibreglass, wickerwork and
foam rubber, among other elements, into her diverse
designs, which included objects for the table, textiles
and jewellery. Ditzel and her husband also published
the book *Danish Chairs* (1954).

The suspended Egg chair is probably Ditzel's most
recognized design. Essentially a hanging armchair,
the Egg was made in natural woven wicker. It could
be suspended from above by a nickel-plated chain
or it could hang on a special steel frame. A separate
covered cushion came with the chair. The Egg is widely
viewed as an example of naturalist Scandinavian
design at its best.

☞ **Items to look out for**

The original Nanna Ditzel
chair can cost upwards of
£2,091 (US $3,560).

Top Tips

Many superstores make
cheaper copies of the
Egg so please check
the provenance carefully
before investing.

Websites

Nanna Ditzel
www.nanna-ditzel.dk

Pierantonio Bonacina
www.pierantoniobonacina.it

Swan Chair
Arne Jacobsen

In the late 1950s, Arne Jacobsen created the Swan Chair and Swan Sofa, among other designs, for the guests of the SAS Royal Hotel in Copenhagen.

The classic Arne Jacobsen design, the Swan Chair, like its brother Swan Sofa and Egg Chair, was created for the magnificent SAS Royal Hotel in Copenhagen. Believing that every element was essential in creating the total effect, Jacobsen paid careful attention to every detail of the furnishings in the hotel – from the lampshades that hung in the lobby, the ashtrays in which guests stubbed out their cigarettes and the lamps under which they read their newspapers. That is part of the reason why so many of the Jacobsen products from that time have entered into design history.

Jacobsen created the Swan Chair primarily for use in the suites, lounges and the panoramic Dining Room on the 25th floor of the hotel. The chair's shell is made of a moulded synthetic material covered by a layer of cold foam, which elegantly rests on an exposed satin-polished aluminium base. The appeal of the chair lies in its curves – rather like those of the Egg Chair.

☞ **Items to look out for**
The original Swan Sofa produced for 10 years between 1964 and '74 by Fritz Hansen.

Top Tips
A more modern licensed version is available in a host of different fabrics and colours. It retails at upwards of £6,000 (US $9,600).

Websites
Fritz Hansen
www.fritzhansen.com

See also
■ Ant, p92
Model 3107, p110
Drop Chair, p136

Cherner Chair
Norman Cherner

The elegant moulded-plywood Cherner Chair is a classic of its time. Recently reissued according to the original specifications, the chair is very popular with collectors.

In 1958 American designer Norman Cherner introduced what was to become a design classic, the Cherner Chair. Cherner had studied and taught in the Fine Arts department of Columbia University. While working as an instructor at the Museum of Modern Art (MoMA) in New York from 1947 to 1949, he also set up his own practice and began to design all kinds of goods, from the furniture, for which he is probably best known, to glassware, lighting and prefabricated housing.

The Cherner Chair is an elegant design. Made of moulded plywood, it comprises a plywood seat made of layers of laminated plywood. The sweeping bentwood arms and legs of the chair add fluidity to the design.

The Cherner Chair Company has reissued all of Norman Cherner's designs, according to the original plans. The company pays the same careful attention to detail in their manufacture as when they were first produced in 1958.

☞ **Items to look out for**

The original model can be found in museum collections.

🕯 **Top Tips**

The reissued chair has been built according to Norman Cherner's original specifications. The armchairs cost about £649–730 (US $999–1,149).

www **Websites**

Cherner Chair Company
www.chernerchair.com

MAA (Swag Leg Chair)
George Nelson

George Nelson produced the Swag Leg Group of chairs, desks and tables in the 1950s. The MAA chair is considered to be one of the most innovative pieces.

A founding father of American modernism, George Nelson designed some of the most original and visually striking furniture of the middle decades of the 20th century. Trained as an architect, Nelson was editor of the magazine *Architectural Forum*. An article on Storagewall, the first modular storage system, brought him to the attention of D.J. DePree, the founder of Herman Miller. He persuaded Nelson to work for the company as his director of design. Nelson also established his own firm, George Nelson & Associates.

In the 1950s Nelson began to toy with the idea of producing furniture with a different kind of sculpted leg. Nelson invented a process, using pressure to curve and bend tubular steel, to produce the swag legs of a range of tables, desks and chairs. The MAA has a moulded-fibreglass seat and back, which sit atop the swag-leg base. A metal-ball-and-rubber-socket connection enables movement. The MAA is popular with collectors.

☞ **Items to look out for**
The 1958 MAA costs c. £500–600 (US $700–800).

🍷 **Top Tips**
Herman Miller reintroduced the MAA as part of its collections.

www **Websites**
George Nelson
www.georgenelson.org

See also
■ Coconut Chair, p108

PK31 Armchair
Poul Kjærholm

Poul Kjærholm struggled to find the ideal form and the PK31 series is possibly the closest he came to it. A freestanding chair, it is classic, elegant and modern.

Poul Kjærholm was one of the most influential Scandinavian designers of the 20th century, his work informing and inspiring that of more modern creative minds such as that of Jasper Morrison.

Among the many classic designs that Kjærholm created, the PK31 Armchair and Sofa Series stands out. The armchair is a prime example of Kjærholm's ability to create furniture that is instantly recognizable as his work and which is both functional and stylish. The designer created the armchair as a self-contained free-standing object in his artistic journey to find the ideal form. The chair defines a cube of 76 centimetres (30 in) on a side, with the seat height at the midpoint. The PK31 Armchair, which features a matt chromed spring-steel base, covered in leather, is all about elegant living. It is also available as two- and three-seater sofas and is manufactured by Fritz Hansen as part of 'The Kjærholm Collection', the designer's work between 1951 and 1967.

☞ **Items to look out for**

The PK31 Armchair can retail from £7,600 (US $11,480).

☞ **Top Tips**

The PK31 is also available as a sofa. It is possible to pick up a modern copy of the armchair for about £731 (US $1,139).

Websites

Fritz Hansen
www.frtizhansen.com

See also

■ PK22, p114

Cone Chair
Verner Panton

Verner Panton prided himself in breaking the mould of what was acceptable design. By using new materials, bright colours and shapes, this designer made his mark on pop culture.

Danish designer Verner Panton's creations can be found in any major design-led home, restaurant or commercial space around the world. Panton's use of new technology and materials to innovate has influenced many top designers in the decades since he was most prolific and his products continue to give people pleasure and inspiration.

The Cone was produced for Panton's first major interior design commission for his parents' Kom-igen inn on the island of Funen. It is a prime example of Panton pushing the boundaries of what was then acceptable design. By creating a pointed swivel-mounted steel base, he immediately posed the question – how would it support the cone-shaped bent-steel seat and frame and also the person sitting in it? The chair's back and seat are formed by a semicircular extension of the shell with wire struts radiating out from the base. Panton produced brightly coloured upholstered and lightly padded versions as well.

☞ **Items to look out for**
The Heart Cone Chair is not the original model but it is a variant of this chair.

💡 **Top Tips**
The Cone range includes upholstered chairs, tables and stools. All available from Vitra.

🌐 **Websites**
Vitra
www.vitra.com

See also
■ Panton Stacking Chair, p166

Drop Chair
Arne Jacobsen

Renaissance man Arne Jacobsen created beautifully designed and constructed highly influential products.
The Drop Chair is a classic example of his art.

One of the early modernists in Scandinavian design, Arne Jacobsen produced some of the most innovative and instantly recognizable designs of the 20th century – from the Swan and Egg Chairs to the Cylinda Tea Service (see *Collectables: 20th-Century Classics*).

One of his most important commissions was the 1958 SAS Royal Hotel in Copenhagen. Asked to complete a total design of the building and its fittings, Jacobsen produced many of the classic designs for which he is most famous – the Swan, the Egg, the AJ Light – for this hotel.

The conical drop chair with its moulded shell was manufactured in limited quantities – only 40 were made – in brown leather with copper legs, for the hotel's Bistro. It was produced by Fritz Hansen. In addition to the 40 chairs for the Bistro, a larger number of Drop Chairs were upholstered in fabric for the bedrooms. Unlike other designs from this period, the Drop Chair was never mass produced.

☞ **Items to look out for**

The brown leather copper-legged chair from the Bistro.

Top Tips

Only 40 chairs were made for the Bistro. These are highly collectable.

You can sit in one if you stay in room 606 at the Radisson Blu Royal Hotel Copenhagen (formerly the SAS Royal Hotel).

Websites

Fritz Hansen
www.fritzhansen.com

See also

Ant, p92
Model 3107, p110
Egg Chair, p122
Swan Chair, p126

Spanish Chair (Model 2226)
Børge Mogensen

Børge Mogensen's designs reveal the classic lines of the materials with which he chose to work. The Spanish Chair is no exception and is quite rustic in feel.

Architect and designer Børge Mogensen designed simple but beautifully constructed furniture and his love of wood and craftsmanship are obvious in all of his work. His designs were inspired from a wide range of influences and are modern interpretations of more traditional pieces. After working as a cabinetmaker, he studied at the Copenhagen School of Arts and Crafts, where he was mentored by the influential Kaare Klint.

In the late 1950s, Mogensen took a trip to Spain, where he became fascinated by the often elaborately carved or decorated chairs found in regions where Islam had been influential – particularly Andalusia, in the south of the country. Mogensen worked on modernizing the design of these chairs, simplifying it to create a clean classic structure with dominant broad armrests. Mogensen's love of wood and clear construction is evident in his Spanish Chair, which has a leather back and seat.

☞ **Items to look out for**
The Spanish Chair can cost from £5,000 (US $8,000) at auction.

Top Tips
A modern version costs about £2,230 (US $3,340).

Websites
Danish Design Store
www.danishdesignstore.com

See also
■ Hunting Chair, p80

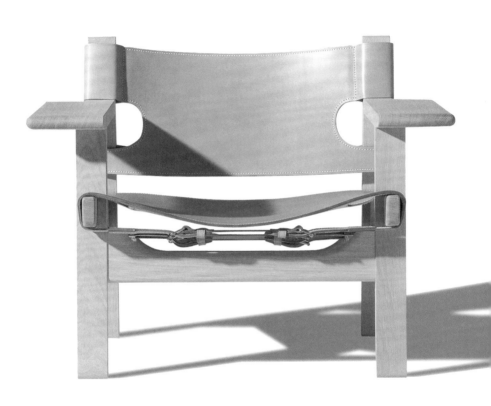

Ox Chair
Hans J. Wegner

Strong and bold yet designed with clean, crisp lines, this 1960 chair is an example of Wegner's belief that furniture can be both functional and beautiful.

Wegner began his career as a cabinetmaker – although he trained to be an architect – and garnered experience working with the influential and much-revered fellow Dane designer Arne Jacobsen before establishing his own office in the early 1940s. He quickly gained a reputation for producing interesting, well-crafted and sometimes irreverent furniture, such as the Valet Chair.

In 1960, Wegner designed the Ox Chair, a padded chair covered with oxhide and raised off the floor by chrome-plated steel legs. Its strong and distinctive design immediately won it fans, as did its resemblance to the shape of a bull and – no less importantly – its comfortableness. It was reported to be Wegner's favourite chair. Johannes Hansen originally made the chair but he ceased its production due to technical problems. It was reissued in 1989 by Erik Jørgensen. To mark the 50th anniversary of the Ox Chair, an exclusive limited edition of the model was made in black, natural or burgundy red vegetable-tanned leather. The seats were numbered and came with a special book.

☞ Items to look out for

The original chair is rare and can go for five figures.

The 50th-anniversary limited edition chair is specially numbered and comes with an anniversary book.

🍴 Top Tips

The Ox Chair is in demand and even modern versions may entail a six-month wait. The leather version retails at about £5,000 (US $8,000). There is also a footstool, or ottoman, available, priced at £1,250 (US $2,000).

🖥 Websites

Danish Design Store
www.danishdesignstore.com

Erik Jørgensen
www.erik-joergensen.com

PK9
Poul Kjærholm

Poul Kjærholm's classic and elegant PK9 chair is also referred to as the 'Tulip', the flower which it so closely resembles. It is very sought after by collectors today.

Although Poul Kjærholm trained as a carpenter he had a great admiration for construction materials as a source for his work. In particular, he liked to work with steel, which he believed was a natural material with many of the same attributes as other natural resources. During his year at the acclaimed company Fritz Hansen, which today produces much of his work in a specific collection, Kjærholm designed many of his most sought-after pieces, several of which feature in this book.

Kjærholm received inspiration for his designs from his surroundings. After seeing the imprint of his wife Hanne's bottom in the sand, the designer became fascinated with the shape. He created the PK9 after asking Hanne to sit in boxes of clay. From this he made the moulding for the leather-covered fibre-reinforced polyester seat. The resulting chair, also known as the 'Tulip', has three thin pieces of satin-brushed stainless steel that act as a column supporting the moulded seat.

☞ **Items to look out for**

The original chair is highly collectable. Don't confuse this with Saarinen's iconic Tulip Chair.

💡 **Top Tips**

Fritz Hansen produces the chair as part of its collection. Available in many colours it retails at about £3,905 (US $6,107).

🌐 **Websites**

Fritz Hansen
www.fritzhansen.com

See also

■ PK22, p114
PK31, p132

Corona Chair (EJ65)
Poul M. Volther

A friend of Hans J. Wegner, Poul M. Volther became famous for his attention-grabbing classic designs such as the highly sought-after Corona Chair.

Like many other Danish designers Poul M. Volther trained as a cabinetmaker and went on to become an architect who created successful design products. He was a great believer in the quality of materials and in craftsmanship. Volther was a good friend of the prolific and influential designer Hans J. Wegner and also worked for FDB from 1949 under Børge Mogensen. He eventually became head of design there.

Volther first conceived the idea for the Corona Chair in 1961, although the prototype had a solid wooden frame. After some experimentation, in 1962, he launched the EJ65 with steel legs and a dual spine, while the four seemingly suspended concentric cushions were made of moulded polyurethane foam upholstered in Italian leather. Manufactured by Erik Jørgensen, the Corona was conceived when Volther apparently saw a time-lapsed photograph of a solar eclipse. The chair combined beauty with ultimate comfort.

☞ **Items to look out for**
The 1961 version with a solid oak frame.

♟ **Top Tips**
There are 'Volther-inspired' versions of this chair available at a much lower price of £600–700 (US $960–1,120).

▭ **Websites**
Skandium
www.skandium.com

Polyprop
Robin Day

The Polyprop chair is probably one of the most familiar
20th-century chairs. A common sight in schools, shops
and businesses, the Polyprop is nonetheless a true classic.

Robin Day and his wife, the acclaimed textile designer
Lucienne Day, were the British equivalents of Charles
and Ray Eames. The Polyprop, which the Days worked
on together, pays more than nod to the Eameses' iconic
fibreglass chairs in terms of style and intent. Robin Day
wanted to produce a stylish mass-market chair that was
cheap and would exploit new technologies – rather as
the Eameses had achieved in post-war United States.

The Polyprop is made of a single piece of injection-
moulded polypropylene (from which it takes its name).
The coloured shell sits squarely on a frame made of
enamelled bent tubular steel. Its splayed legs were
similar to other designs of the time – such as those
of British designer Ernest Race. Polypropylene is an
inexpensive, durable and easy to clean material. A
single injection mould can produce about 4,000
shells per week. Since Hille International started
manufacturing it in 1963, the Polyprop has sold more
than 14 million units globally.

☞ **Items to look out for**

The original chairs
were produced by Hille
International and bear
the stamp.

💡 **Top Tips**

**This chair has been
endlessly copied** so do
check to see if it is an original
Day Polyprop.

🌐 **Websites**

Design Museum
www.designmuseum.org

Scimitar Chair
Fabricius and Kastholm

The extremely rare Scimitar Chair takes its name from a Turkish sword. Made of steel and leather it was the result of a collaboration between two leading designers.

Architect and furniture designer Jørgen Kastholm met the architect Preben Fabricius at the School of Interior Design in Copenhagen. Kastholm was employed by Fritz Hansen after leaving college; Fabricius had previously served as an apprentice to master cabinetmaker Niels Vodder, and after finishing at the School was employed by architect Ole Hagen. From 1961, Fabricius and Kastholm collaborated to create low-cost housing and a range of truly unique furniture. The 1963 Scimitar Chair (or Horseshoe Chair) was part of this line.

The manufacture of the chair initially proved difficult. The three-section base was created by pouring hot metal into individual ceramic moulds. The sections were then welded into shape. Many companies turned the job down but eventually Ivan Schlechter agreed to take it on. The Scimitar was first exhibited in 1963 at the Copenhagen Museum of Industrial Arts to great acclaim.

 Items to look out for

It is possible to pick up a Scimitar Chair at auction for as little as £3,190–3,830 (US $5–6,000).

 Top Tips

Today you can buy the chair, which Lange Production has the rights to produce, along with other products by the design team.

 Websites

Lange Production
www.langeproduction.com

Shell Chair (CH07)
Hans J. Wegner

Hans J. Wegner's chairs are among the most collectable in the world. This prolific designer's work combines brilliant craftsmanship with simplicity and elegance.

Hans J. Wegner's chairs helped put mid-20th-century Danish design on the international map and also popularized it, making stylish furniture available to people who otherwise wouldn't have been able to afford the cost. He is considered to be the finest of the Scandinavian cabinetmakers and made fully functional furniture that was beautifully crafted and manufactured. His work is timeless.

The Shell Chair, or CH07, created in 1963, is one of the designer's most interesting chairs. The chair's curving seat supported by three legs makes it instantly recognizable. It almost disappeared into obscurity but in the early 1990s, Carl Hansen and Son re-released the Shell. The wing-like design of the seat has also led it to be called the 'Smiling Chair'.

Today the Danish Design Store offers the chair in many different colours and finishes. These include the Limited Edition Wegner CH07 Shell Chair, of which only 250 were ever made. On the underside of each chair is a sterling silver plate with a number.

☞ **Items to look out for**
An original Shell Chair sold at Christie's for £20,000 (US $31,290).

🍗 **Top Tips**
A limited edition chair costs £4,154 (US $6,500).

▦ **Websites**
Danish Design Store
www.danishdesignstore.com

See also
■ Round Chair, p68
Wishbone Chair, p72
Folding Chair, p76
■ Flag Halyard, p82
Teddy Bear Chair, p86
■ Ox Chair, p140
■ The Circle Chair, p182

Lounge Chair
Grete Jalk

Featured in design collections around the world, including MoMA in New York, Grete Jalk's fascinating plywood chair challenges perceptions of what good design is.

Architect and furniture designer Grete Jalk is one of the few successful women from the predominantly male world of Danish design. In the 1960s at the Copenhagen Cabinetmakers' Guild Exhibition, a leading critic referred to her as a fine example of 'the strong weaker sex'! Her work is both unique and individualistic, and Jalk has garnered great critical acclaim internationally.

Jalk trained at the School of Arts and Crafts, before studying with the influential designer Kaare Klint at the Royal Academy of Fine Arts. After setting up her own design studio, she made a name for herself through her designs for Fritz Hansen and Poul Jeppesen. After winning several awards, Jalk designed the Lounge Chair – a moulded bent teak-faced plywood chair – for Poul Jeppesen. It was groundbreaking to the degree to which the plywood had been bent over a single plane. Only 300 were originally made and despite winning a British award, it never went into mass production.

☞ Items to look out for

The original model was manufactured by Poul Jeppesen. Only 300 were made.

♟ Top Tips

Lange Production makes the chair (GJ Chair) in its original wood specifications – teak and Oregon pine. Each piece is stamped and dated.

▭ Websites

Lange Production
www.langeproduction.com

Djinn Chaise Longue
Olivier Mourgue

Olivier Mourgue's Djinn Series became famous when the chair featured in Stanley Kubrick's groundbreaking film *2001: A Space Odyssey*. The chaise longue was the first in the series.

French designer Olivier Mourgue was born in 1939 in Paris. He is a talented painter, industrial designer and landscape architect. After studying interior design in Paris, the Frenchman gained invaluable experience studying and working in Finland and Sweden. From 1963, Mourgue's designs – including the Djinn Series – were produced by French manufacturer Airborne International. The classic chair rose to prominence after it appeared in *2001: A Space Odyssey*.

The Djinn Chaise Longue, designed in 1963, was the first in the Djinn Series. Its undulating tubular steel-frame seat and trestle ends rest on exposed steel bands. The frame of the low chaise was covered in polyurethane foam and upholstered with stretch jersey fabric. Mourgue named it after the supernatural djinn that feature in ancient Persian, Indian and Arabic mythology. The djinn have a humanlike shape and can take on the form of animals for short periods.

☞ **Items to look out for**
The Djinn Chaise Longue can be found at auction for as little as £1,000 (US $1,558).

🍴 **Top Tips**
More modern versions are available in different colours.

🌐 **Websites**
Olivier Mourgue
www.oliviermourgue.com

Karuselli Chair
Yrjö Kukkapuro

Yrjö Kukkapuro's Karuselli Chair was named the world's most comfortable chair by the *New York Times* in 1974, even though the chair had been designed a decade earlier.

Finnish-born designer Yrjö Kukkapuro believes that there should be three key elements present in successful furniture design – ecology, ergonomics and aesthetics – and he has worked hard over the decades to make sure his striking creations meet those criteria.

Kukkapuro, who was a former principal and professor at the University of Art and Design in Helsinki, is known most prominently for a series of original and visually challenging chairs. The Karuselli Chair, designed in 1964, has a leather-upholstered foam-covered seat shell and base made of moulded white fibreglass. The shell is connected to the cruciform swivel base by a chrome steel spring and rubber damper.

Kukkapuro was inspired to design the chair after making snow seats with his daughter, Isa. The Karuselli Chair is reported to be one of British designer Sir Terence Conran's favourite pieces.

☞ **Items to look out for**

The Karuselli Chair is available from high-end shops such as The Conran Shop for upwards of £4,000 (US $6,200).

💡 **Top Tips**

A sticker on the bottom of the chair says 'Avarte. Made in Finland, designed by Yrjö Kukkapuro. Designed in 1964.'

Don't get confused with the miniature version which costs about £485 (US $680).

💻 **Websites**

Conran Shop
www.conranshop.com

Elda Chair
Joe Colombo

1964

During Joe Colombo's relatively short life he produced some of the most interesting and inspiring industrial designs that the world has seen. The Elda Chair is just one of them.

Fans of the sci-fi series Space 1999 will recognize Joe Colombo's Elda Chair from the 1970s' series. A 20th-century classic, Colombo's chair combines comfort with the space-age feel so fashionable in the early 1960s.

Italian-born Colombo designed the chair in about 1964. It was one of the first large armchairs to have a frame made of fibreglass-reinforced polyester. It was all about comfort and was a chair that the user could literally sink into. The leather-covered foam upholstery was bolstered further by seven fat sausagelike cushions attached by metal hooks. The fibreglass frame also sat on a metal swivelling mechanism that made it easy for the user to adjust his or her position for the most comfort. Joe Colombo died of a heart attack at the tragically early age of 41. He believed his designs were all about creating an environment for the future and through designs such as the Elda and Birillo he achieved that aim.

☞ **Items to look out for**
The 1964 chair is highly collectable, especially to fans of *Space 1999*.

🕯 **Top Tips**
For a long time the chair was not available in the UK. It now retails for about £4,329 (US $6,280).

▭ **Websites**
Joe Colombo Studio
www.joecolombo.com
Twenty Twentyone
www.twentytwentyone.com

See also
■ Birillo, p172

Ribbon Chair
Pierre Paulin

Featured in the cult British sci-fi series *Space 1999*, Pierre Paulin's stunning Ribbon Chair was created in 1965. It subsequently won the Chicago Design Award.

French designer Pierre Paulin stated that 'A chair should be more than simply functional. It should be friendly, fun and colourful.' His Ribbon Chair, deemed by many to be one of the most comfortable chairs ever made, is proof that Paulin put his money where his mouth was!

Paulin began designing furniture for Thonet. In the late 1950s, he joined Artifort, designing a series of chairs with an inner structure of steel tubing covered in foam and fabric. The Ribbon Chair was created for the company in 1965. It comprises a tubular steel frame with horizontal springs covered by moulded foam and upholstered in any number of fabrics. The base of the chair is lacquered pressed wood. Considered by some to be one of the most beautiful chairs in the world, the Ribbon is an acquired taste. Some critics find its unconventional shape too much to take, but the chair's contoured form is specially designed to enable the user to assume a variety of positions while still being given essential support.

☞ **Items to look out for**
The **1966 model** made for Artifort.

One of the Ribbon Chairs featured in *Space 1999*.

💡 **Top Tips**
Available in several colours and fabrics the Ribbon Chair costs about £6,500 (US $10,400). A matching Ribbon Ottoman is also available.

www **Websites**
Artifort
www.artifort.com

Ball (Globe) Chair
Eero Aarnio

1966

One of the most recognizable chairs of the 1960s, the Ball Chair has appeared in many films and in the designer Vivienne Westwood's fashion shows.

The sculptural beauty of the Ball Chair helped turn it into a much sought-after design classic. Designer, Eero Aarnio was born in 1932. After studying at the Institute of Industrial Arts in Helsinki, he began to produce groundbreaking designs; he established his own office in 1962. The idea for the Ball Chair originated in 1963, when the designer could not find the right 'big' chair for his home and he then decided to make his own. He said: 'After some drawing I noticed that the shape of the chair had become so simple that it was merely a ball.' He determined the height of the chair by pinning a full-scale drawing to a wall and 'sitting' in it, while his wife drew around his head. Aarnio made the prototype by creating an inner plywood body mould, which he then covered with wet paper. After laminating the surface with fibreglass, he removed the mould and had it upholstered, adding a leg and thus 'The Ball Chair was born.'

☞ **Items to look out for**

The original Ball Chair has a red telephone on the inside wall.

♟ **Top Tips**

Be wary of fakes. Don't mistake the Ball Chair for the Sphere Chair, the unauthorized copy.

🌐 **Websites**

Eero Aarnio
www.eero-aarnio.com
Adelta
www.adelta.de

See also
■ Bubble Chair p168

PK24 Chaise Longue (Hammock)
Poul Kjærholm

Kjærholm is known for his clean, elegant modernist furniture made with an incredible attention to detail. The PK24 Chaise Longue is also known as the 'Hammock'.

Trained as a carpenter, Poul Kjærholm graduated from the Copenhagen School of Arts and Crafts in the early 1950s. He loved experimenting with construction materials, particularly steel. He said: 'Steel's constructive potential is not the only thing that interests me; the refraction of light on its surface is an important part of my ... work. I consider steel a material with the same artistic merit as wood and leather.'

The characteristic style of Kjærholm's work – clean and elegant lines and the fine attention to even the smallest detail – was evident at an early stage of his career. In creating the PK24, or the 'Hammock' as he referred to it, Kjærholm was influenced by the rococo period and the idea of the French long chair. In the original design, the wicker seat actually has no physical connection with the satin-brushed stainless-steel base. These two parts are kept together by gravity and the friction between them.

☞ **Items to look out for**
The PK24 can cost as much as £14,000 (US $22,400).

💡 **Top Tips**
More modern versions are available in leather or wicker and both come with a headrest.

Websites
Fritz Hansen
www.fritzhansen.com

See also
■ PK22, p114
PK31, p132
■ PK9, p142

Panton Stacking Chair
Verner Panton

Stylish, sexy and fun, the Panton Stacking Chair made its first appearance in 1967. Now instantly recognizable, the chair is probably the most famous of Panton's many iconic designs.

Remembered for the use of psychedelic colours, space-age design and modern materials in his many products, Verner Panton designed the Panton Stacking Chair in 1960, but it had to wait seven years before going into production. When the chair made its first appearance in 1967 in the Danish magazine *Mobilia*, it instantly created a huge storm. Its sleek, colourful curved design and the groundbreaking idea of a cantilever chair made from one continuous piece of plastic immediately grabbed the imagination of critics and audiences alike.

With the help of Vitra technicians, Panton and owner Willi Fehlbaum developed the chair from its original 1960 concept to one better suited to a mass-market audience. It was first produced in polyester resin reinforced with fibreglass and then later in polyurethane rigid foam. The current model is made from rigid expanded polypropylene with a lacquered surface.

☞ **Items to look out for**
The original chairs made of polyester resin reinforced with fibreglass.

Top Tips
The Panton Stacking Chair retails from £834 (US $1,335). It is made from rigid expanded plastic with a lacquered surface. A cheaper version also exists made of lower-grade plastic.

Websites
Skandium
www.skandium.com
Vitra
www.vitra.com

See also
■ Cone Chair, p134

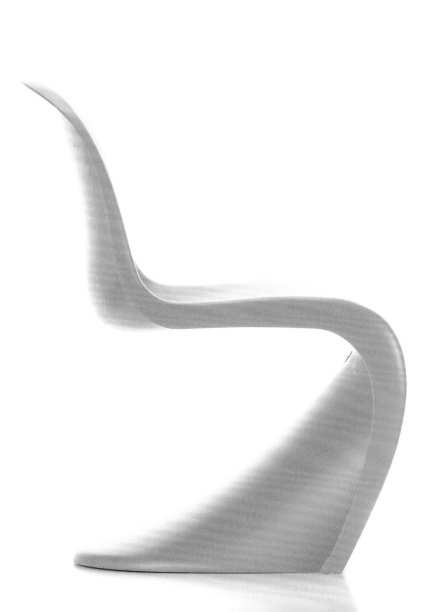

Bubble Chair
Eero Aarnio

Mixing space-age design with fun, the Bubble Chair challenged ideas of what a chair should be and do. Based on Aarnio's earlier Ball Chair, it is clear like a soap bubble.

The Finnish designer Eero Aarnio is the master of using industrial plastics in modern domestic design.

After establishing his own studio in 1962, Aarnio began to experiment with materials. First came the Ball Chair, a 'room within a room', which was upholstered in foam. Aarnio wanted to produce a chair with more light. Working on the design, he came up with the Bubble Chair, in which the user could sit cocooned in a sphere while still being aware of the world through its transparent walls.

He commented: 'The only suitable material is acrylic, which is heated and blown into a shape like a soap bubble. Since I knew that the dome-shaped skylights are made in this way, I contacted the manufacturer and asked if it would be technically possible to blow a bubble that is bigger than a hemisphere.... I had a steel ring made, the bubble was blown and cushions were added and the chair was ready.

'And, again, the name was obvious: BUBBLE.'

☞ **Items to look out for**
The Bubble Chair can cost upwards of £5,000 (US $8,000).

🍽 **Top Tips**
Nanna Ditzel's Egg is often confused with the Bubble Chair. The Egg is an earlier design.

There are very many fakes on the market. Look carefully at the provenance of the chair.

💻 **Websites**
Danish Design Store
www.danishdesignstore.com
PP Møbler
www.ppdk.com

Soft Pad
Charles and Ray Eames

Fearlessly adventurous, husband-and-wife team Charles and Ray Eames pushed the boundaries of design, creating some of the most iconic yet practical chairs, including the Soft Pad.

The association between Charles and Ray Eames and furniture manufacturer Herman Miller proved a commercially lucrative and innovative success.

The Soft Pad came about through the creation of the Eameses' earlier EA111 Aluminium Chair. Architect, designer and friend Eero Saarinen asked the pair to design a high-quality outdoor chair for the industrialist J. Irwin Miller's home. The result was a chair made from cast aluminium with an innovative seat-back suspension. It was a major departure from the concept of the chair as a solid shell. In 1958, Herman Miller began manufacturing the EA111 Aluminium Chair, which was praised for its intelligent use of materials and the fact that the seat and back readily adapted to the shape of the person sitting in it without needing extra upholstery. In 1968, the couple extended the range by adding plush cushions to the frame. The Soft Pad, as it is now known, is made of 60 percent recycled materials and 90 percent of the chair is recyclable.

☞ **Items to look out for**
The original 1969 model.

🍋 **Top Tips**
A modern version is sold by Herman Miller and Vitra for about £2,500 (US $4,000) without arms (known as the Side Chair). Arms cost an additional £155 (US $250).

🖵 **Websites**
Herman Miller
www.hermanmiller.com
Vitra: www.vitra.com

See also

▧ Moulded Plywood Chairs, p60
  La Chaise, p64
  LAR, DAR, RAR, p66

■ DSX, DSW and DSR, p84
  Model 670 and 671, p116

Birillo
Joe Colombo

During his 41-year life, Joe Colombo designed some very groundbreaking furniture and lighting. The Birillo bar stool was featured in the 1982 sci-fi classic movie *Blade Runner*.

Born in Italy, talented designer Joe Colombo strived throughout his short life to create the environment of the future. He continuously evolved as a designer, grasping new material, new technologies and challenging existing boundaries to create new designs, such as the Elda, the first armchair to be made from fibreglass at such a size, and the Additional Living System, which consisted of six-differently sized moulded-polyurethane cushions that could be put together in different configurations by the user. In the 1960s, Colombo created Box 1 'night and day facility' – a series of interlocking boxes that contained the contents of a conventional bedroom and when divided became a bed, shelves and a wardrobe.

In 1970–1 Colombo produced the Birillo (Barstool) as part of Visiona, his 'habitat of the future'. The leather revolving seat and back sat atop a single tubular chrome-plated steel leg, which was supported by a fibreglass base that hid castors.

☞ Items to look out for

For the 40th anniversary Zanotta produced a special-edition version of the Birillo.

🔩 Top Tips

Joe Colombo's chair is manufactured by Zanotta today. It is available in white, barley and black.

You can pick one up for about £2,111 (US $3,289).

🖥 Websites

Bonluxat
www.bonluxat.com

See also
◼ Elda Chair, p158

Easy Edges Series
Frank O. Gehry

Always an innovator, architect Frank O. Gehry captured the design world's attention with his Easy Edges Series – created from the reuse of corrugated cardboard.

In the 1960s architect Frank O. Gehry began to experiment with different materials for his furniture. Using an everyday product, corrugated cardboard, he began to 'play with it, to glue it together and to cut it into shapes with a handsaw and a pocket knife.' His experiments were successful and Gehry used the material – utilizing about 60 layers of cardboard screwed and glued together and moulded to create fluid lines – to create his influential Easy Edges Series of furniture.

All of the pieces in the Easy Edges collection, including the Wiggle Side Chair and the Easy Edges Lounge Chair (opposite), appear playful and effortless in their execution. In fact what they really do is showcase Gehry's dedication to skilled craftsmanship and functional engineering. The series also demonstrates that he was, yet again, ahead of the game. Decades before eco design became fashionable, Gehry was reusing a commonly found material to create his furniture.

☞ **Items to look out for**
The originals can be found in design museums around the world.

♟ **Top Tips**
Vitra has begun to reproduce some of the Easy Edges Series, including the Wiggle Side Chair, Stool and Table. They are available in corrugated cardboard and natural hardboard.

▭ **Websites**
Vitra
www.vitra.com

See also
■ Power Play Club Chair, p192

Wink Lounge Chair
Toshiyuki Kita

Toshiyuki Kita produced the ergonomic Wink Lounge Chair in 1980. He says that a good designer should always think of the consumer, the distributor and the manufacturer.

Japanese furniture and product designer Toshiyuki Kita was born in 1942 in the city of Osaka. After graduating from the Naniwa Design College, he worked for an aluminium company. Interested in combining contemporary design with traditional handcrafted work, he opened a design office in Japan in 1967 to produce his own furniture. He later opened an office in Italy. Kita has worked with many international companies, including Cassina, Sharp and Mitsubishi, since then.

In 1980 he designed the ergonomic and extremely clever Wink Lounge Chair. Reminiscent of a car seat, the Wink can be used either as a lounge recliner or a chair. Made of a steel frame with a CFC-free polyurethane foam and polyester wadding, the chair is usually upholstered in leather or fabric. Side knobs allow the back to be adjusted. By tilting the base forward the chair becomes a chaise longue. The headrest is divided into two parts, each with its own reclining action.

☞ **Items to look out for**

The Wink can be found in the permanent collections of leading museums such as the Pompidou in Paris.

💡 **Top Tips**

Cassina is the official distributor of the Wink Lounge Chair. It retails at about £1,300 (US $2,300).

www **Websites**

Cassina
www.cassina.com
Toshiyuki Kita's site
www.toshiyukikita.com

Rover Chair
Ron Arad

The Rover Chair was the first piece of furniture that influential industrial designer Ron Arad produced. His fun but functional products often mix the old with the new.

Israeli-born Ron Arad is considered to be one of the influential industrial designers of our time. His fun, functional yet innovative products merge playfulness and whimsy often with cutting edge technology. After training as an architect at the Bezalel Academy of Art and Design in Jerusalem and later in London at the Architectural Association, Arad set up the company One Off Ltd in London.

Arad made the Rover Chair after experimenting with some abandoned car seats and discarded pieces of metal that he picked up in a scrapyard in North London. He mounted a seat from a Rover 200 car onto a curved metal frame taken from a 1930s' milking parlour and the Rover Chair was born. Arad put them up for sale in his Covent Garden shop. One day a Frenchman turned up wanting to buy six at £99 each, more than three times what they had cost to make – the man was French fashion designer Jean Paul Gaultier and the chair subsequently became a bestseller.

☞ **Items to look out for**
A 1981 Rover Chair, produced by One Off, recently sold at Bonhams for £3,240 (US $5,480).

❢ **Top Tips**
The Rover Chair has an adjustable back and Kee-Klamp fittings.

www **Websites**
Ron Arad site
www.ronarad.com

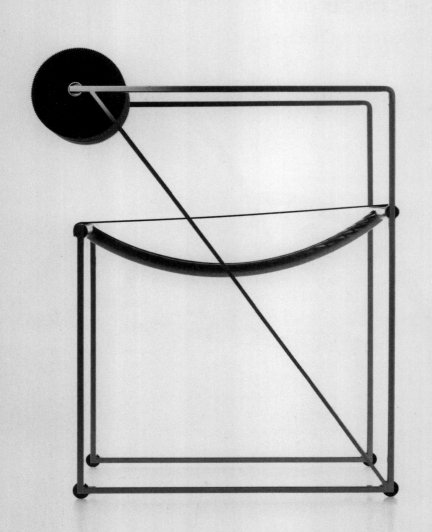

Seconda 602
Mario Botta

Like many other eminent industrial designers, Mario Botta originally trained as an architect before going on to make furniture and industrial design products.

Swiss-born Mario Botta studied at the Academy of Fine Arts in Milan and at the University of Venice. After graduating he worked for Le Corbusier before opening an architectural practice in Lugano. Over the years buildings such as the Cathedral at Evry (1988–90) and the San Francisco Museum of Modern Art (1990–5) have cemented the Swiss designer's reputation as a leading exponent of the 'Ticino School'. From the early 1980s Botta designed lighting and furniture. For Alias he produced a series of chairs, including the Prima, Seconda and Terzo Series. The Seconda 602 has become a design classic.

Produced in 1982, the chair pays more than a nod to Bauhaus. Its frame is made out of stove-enamelled steel, as is its seat, which is in stove-enamelled perforated steel. The Seconda 602's back consists of two black polyurethane cylindrical elements. The chair can be found in leading design museums around the world.

☞ **Items to look out for**
Look for the Seconda in Botta's various buildings.

🍋 **Top Tips**
The chair costs about £898 (US $1,400).

▭ **Websites**
Ambiente Direct www.ambientedirect.com

The Circle Chair (PP130)
Hans J. Wegner

Like the Flag Halyard, the Circle Chair seems to be completely unlike any of Hans J. Wegner's historic chair designs. It thus illustrates his creative genius and range.

By the time that Hans J. Wegner conceived the Circle, he had produced hundreds of chairs, most bearing the instantly recognizable Wegner design stamp. The Circle Chair and its predecessor, the Flag Halyard, show that Wegner's innovative creative spirit was still present.

Although Wegner loved wood and was known for the time he dedicated to shaping and sanding his designs, he originally conceived the main structure, the circle, to be made from bent iron. In the end, however, master of crafts Søren Holst Pedersen and master journeyman Henry Fisker at PP Møbler developed a special machine for manufacturing the hoop circle that forms the mass of the design of the chair in wood.

The Circle Chair utilizes factors present in many of the other chairs produced by the designer – soap-treated solid ash in its frame and the plaited flag line. It was produced from 1986 onwards.

☞ **Items to look out for**
The original chair in ash.

🍵 **Top Tips**
Expect to pay £4,525 (US $7,700) upwards for a natural soap-treated ash-framed chair.

Websites
Skandium
www.skandium.com

See also
- Round Chair, p68
  Wishbone Chair, p72
  Folding Chair, p76
- Flag Halyard, p82
  Teddy Bear Chair, p86
  Sawhorse Easy Chair, p94
  Cow Horn Chair, p96
  Valet Chair, p102
- Ox Chair, p140
  Shell Chair, p150

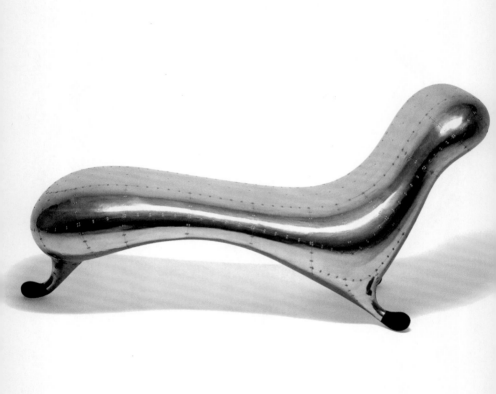

Lockheed Lounge
Marc Newson

Marc Newson's designs have become very collectable in recent years. The lovely fluid lines of the Lockheed Lounge have attracted young collectors around the world.

Australian-born designer Marc Newson has won numerous awards for his innovative designs – which range from bicycles and cars to luggage and sunglasses. He has worked for most of the world's leading international brands, including Samsonite, Ford, Cappellini and Alessi.

Born in Sydney in 1963, Newson was exposed to good design at an early age through his mother who was the manager of a beachfront hotel. Newson recalls that he saw 'all this really cool Italian stuff: Joe Colombo trolleys and Sacco beanbags'. He went on to study jewellery and sculpture.

In 1986 he made the piece that would establish his name, the Lockheed Lounge. Loosely derived from 18th-century chaises longues that he had seen in paintings, Newson painstakingly created the piece from hammering hundreds of industrial aluminium panels onto a home-made fibreglass mould. Newson described it as a 'a fluid metallic form like a giant blob of mercury'.

☞ **Items to look out for**
The Lockheed Lounge recently sold at auction for a staggering £960,000 (US $1.5 million).

🍦 **Top Tips**
Marc Newson's work is very collectable. Look out for his smaller, more affordable pieces.

www **Websites**
Marc Newson
www.marc-newson.com

How High the Moon
Shiro Kuramata

Shiro Kuramata turned everyday industrial materials into beautiful functional objects. This chair, made of steel mesh, borrows its name from a Duke Ellington song.

Shiro Kuramata was one of the most influential Japanese industrial designers of the 20th century. Through mesmerizing pieces such as Glass Chair (1976) and How High the Moon (1986) he challenged perceptions of what good design should be and inspired a whole generation of younger designers. His work forms part of the collections of leading museums around the world.

Born in Tokyo in 1934, he studied western interior design, later working for a small department store San-Ai, designing its floor and window displays and as a freelance designer for Matsuy, before he opened his own office in 1965.

How High the Moon was conceived in the 1980s. Made from nickel-plated steel mesh, a material usually associated with industrial product and mostly kept out of view, the chair has a streamlined elegance. The shimmering silver quality of the perforated mesh creates an airy, light feel. The chair is both functional and beautiful.

☞ **Items to look out for**
The 1986 chair has sold at auction for about £27,000 (US $42,000).

● **Top Tips**
Check the dimensions carefully as miniature chairs are available.

▭ **Websites**
Shiro Kuramata
www.shirokuramata.com

Thinking Man's Chair
Jasper Morrison

British designer Jasper Morrison has created products for some of the leading companies in the world – from Flos and Rosenthal to Cappellini and Alessi.

London-born Jasper Morrison studied at the prestigious Royal College of Art and on scholarship at the former HdK Berlin (today the Universität der Künste Berlin) before setting up Office for Design in his hometown. Morrison's work has been featured in exhibitions around the world and internationally renowned companies such as Flos, SCP and Alessi include his designs among their collections.

In 1986, Morrison created the elegant Thinking Man's Chair, which harps back to the Functionalist metal furniture of the early 20th century, for an exhibition in Japan. The chair was subsequently distributed by Cappellini.

Morrison originally named his concept the Drinking Man's Chair. The metal disks at the end of the curved arms were meant to hold drinking vessels. He renamed it the Thinking Man's Chair after he made a model of the chair from pipe cleaners. The slogan 'The Thinking Man's Smoke' was on the pipe-cleaner packet.

☞ **Items to look out for**
The original model made of welded and painted tubular steel and strip metal can be found in design collections worldwide, including the Victoria and Albert Museum in London.

Top Tips
The early chairs had the dimensions of different metal elements painted onto them. Cappellini omitted this on its version. They retail for £1,465–1,522 (US $ 2,282–2,443).

Websites
Jasper Morrison
www.jaspermorrison.com

See also
▪ Low Pad, p200

S Chair
Tom Dixon

A chair that pays more than a nod to Verner Panton's classic Stacking Chair, Tom Dixon's S Chair uses natural materials to create a product that is less industrial and more organic.

Self-taught British designer Tom Dixon experiments with texture and materials to create very interesting and innovative work. Pieces of his furniture such as the S Chair, designed in 1988, showcase Dixon's distinctive style, as well as referencing outside influences. The cantilevered structure of early Marcel Breuer chairs, the curves of the Panton Stacking Chair and even African traditional craftwork are all evident in the design of his S Chair. Dixon, who handcrafted the chair, made more than 50 prototypes using different materials, including rubber and paper, before he decided to use two types of covering: gnarled woven marsh straw and wicker. The frame of the S Chair is made of dark lacquered metal and is stabilized by a circular base. The S Chair appealed to a specific design market, as catered to by Italian furniture manufacturer Cappellini, which eventually put the chair into mass production.

☞ **Items to look out for**
The original S Chair was made in woven marsh straw or wicker. Later models have different coverings.

♟ **Top Tips**
There are limited-edition versions made by Cappellini such as the 2003 version, which uses a deconstruction of the company's trademark to decorate the chair.

▭ **Websites**
Cappellini
www.cappellini.it
Tom Dixon
www.tomdixon.net

See also
◼ Bird Chaise Longue, p198

Power Play Club Chair
Frank O. Gehry

Most people link the name 'Frank Gehry' with the extraordinary architecture of such buildings as the Bilbao Guggenheim Museum, but he also designs furniture.

Frank Gehry is one of the most influential architects working today. His buildings grace the landscapes of the world's most important cities. Throughout, Gehry has always designed furniture. His first series, Easy Edges, was conceived between 1969 and 1973 and combined playfulness with an almost faultless precision. It utilized engineering techniques to make the work structurally functional. These were more than just pieces of whimsy on Gehry's part.

In 1989 Knoll approached Gehry to ask him to design furniture. He asked Knoll to create a studio for him along the lines of that used by Charles and Ray Eames. The Power Play Series, designed in 1991, took its inspiration from Gehry's youth and was based on the apple crates that he played with as a child. The Power Play Club Chair (and Ottoman) are made of curvilinear laminated maple, for the most part fashioned with ribbonlike waving strips of wood. The Club Chair is high-backed with arms. It is designed for comfort as well as beauty.

Items to look out for
Each Knoll chair features an official studio logo, Gehry's signature and the date of production.

Top Tips
The chair retails from £4,500 (US $7,450). The ottoman is priced at £1,450 (US $2,233). A fish-shaped cushion snaps on underneath the chair.

Websites
Knoll
www.knoll.com

See also
■ Easy Edges Series, p174

Louis 20 Chair
Philippe Starck

Philippe Starck's work combines humour, versatility and innovation. It challenges the viewer – whether the piece be a three-legged chair or a lobster-shaped lemon squeezer.

Philippe Starck's designs inform the modern world and the modern way of living – whether it be through an Alessi corkscrew or a three-legged chair most people are aware of this great French designer's challenging work. Always beautifully constructed, Starck combines materials never used before, bright colours, odd shapes and so much more, and in doing so he continually challenges our perceptions of acceptable design.

The Louis 20 Chair takes its name from the French Kings who were often only distinguishable from each other by the number at the end of their name. The chair came about after protracted technical experiments by the engineers of Swiss furniture manufacturer Vitra and the designer. The chair that evolved combined a shell and two legs made from one piece of blown polypropylene with a perhaps incongruous pair of aluminium legs, which were joined to the body by a plate that allowed it to be tilted on its back legs.

☞ **Items to look out for**
The chair also comes with aluminium arms.

💧 **Top Tips**
Don't buy a miniature Louis 20 – unless that's your intention.

🌐 **Websites**
Vitra
www.vitra.com

Balzac Armchair and Ottoman
Matthew Hilton

When British designer Matthew Hilton created the Balzac Armchair
and Ottoman for the design retailer SCP in 1991,
they were an instant success.

British designer Matthew Hilton was born in Hastings,
Sussex, in 1957. He studied furniture design at Kingston
Polytechnic in the 1970s and after graduating began
designing and manufacturing low-tech cast metal
objects. His products achieved some recognition
when British fashion retailer Paul Smith and French
company Joseph Pour La Maison sold them in their
London showrooms.

In the mid-1980s, Hilton established his own self-
named company and began a collaboration
with manufacturer and cutting-edge British retailer
SCP. Now Based in Shoreditch, East London, SCP
released their first Hilton-designed pieces, the Balzac
Armchair and Ottoman, in 1991.

The Balzac has a solid beech frame with steel springs
and elasticated webbing, covered in multi-density
foam with a feather cushion and American oak legs.
Full of comfortable curves and encased in soft aniline
leather, the Balzac Armchair helped establish Hilton's
reputation as a designer.

☞ Items to look out for

The original Balzac
Armchair and Ottoman
retail at about £3,030
(US $4,850).

🍸 Top Tips

The Balzac Armchair can
be bought separately for
£2,798 (US $4,480).

It is possible to buy Two-
and Three-Seater Balzac
Sofas.

💻 Websites

Heal's
www.heals.co.uk
SCP
www.scp.co.uk

Bird Chaise Longue
Tom Dixon

1991

Tom Dixon fell into design after a motorcycle accident left him with time on his hands. Since then he has become a leading light in world design and is creative head of Artek.

Born in Tunisia, Dixon grew up in London. After dropping out of art school and playing in a band called Funkapolitan, Dixon taught himself design while trying to weld together his motorbike. He sold his early welded products and eventually opened a shop to market his designs. He later allowed the company Eurolounge to manufacture his products. He also collaborated with other designers and, in his role as head of design for the company Habitat, he reissued the designs of Verner Panton and Robin Day. He is now creative director of Artek, the very successful company founded by Alvar Aalto and his wife to sell their lovely work.

The Bird Chaise Longue is a fun and functional design, combining elements of a classic chaise longue with that of a see-saw chair. An extremely comfortable chair, it allows the user to rest on his/her centre of gravity or to rock. Made of an upholstered wooden structure, it has removable covers available in a host of colours.

☞ **Items to look out for**
The original chaise is very collectable.

💡 **Top Tips**
A modern version of the Bird Chaise Longue costs about £2,224 (US $3,465).

🌐 **Websites**
Cappellini
www.cappellini.it

See also
■ S Chair, p190

Low Pad
Jasper Morrison

English designer Jasper Morrison's stylishly comfortable Low Pad was inspired by one of his favourite chairs, Poul Kjaerholm's 1956 PK22 (see p114).

Born in London in 1959, Jasper Morrison attended Kingston Polytechnic Design School and the Royal College of Art in London before winning a scholarship to study at HdK Berlin.

In the mid-1980s, Morrison set up a design office in London. He began to attract attention when he collaborated with several leading international companies, including the East London-based design company SCP, the office-furniture company Vitra and the Italian furniture producer Cappellini, which produced his chair the Low Pad.

Morrison's chair combines style and comfort with sleek design. Essentially an armchair that can exist with or without arms, it is made with a plywood and multi-density polyurethane foam seat. The chair can be covered in fabric or leather and is suitable for office use or in a design-conscious home. The chair's legs are made of satined stainless steel and have rubber feet.

Items to look out for
The Low Pad retails at about £835 (US $1,335).

Top Tips
The Low Pad is available with or without arms and can be covered in fabric or leather.

Websites
Cappellini
www.cappellini.it
Jasper Morrison Products
www.jaspermorrison.com

See also
■ Thinking Man's Chair, p188

Notes on Designers

Alvar Aalto (1898–1976) Finnish architect and furniture designer. *See:* 41 Paimio; Model No. 31 (Cantilever Chair); No. 60 (Stacking Stool).

Eero Aarnio (1932–) Finnish furniture designer. *See:* Ball (Globe) Chair; Bubble Chair.

Ron Arad (1951–) British–Israeli architect and product designer. *See:* Rover Chair.

Harry Bertoia (1915–1978) Italian-born American furniture designer. *See:* Diamond Chair; Bird Chair and Ottoman.

Mario Botta (1943–) Swiss architect and furniture designer. *See:* Seconda 602.

Marcel Breuer (1902–81) Hungarian-born American architect and furniture designer. *See:* B3 (Wassily Chair); B32; Isokon Long Chair.

Achille (1918–2002) and **Pier Giacomo Castiglioni** (1913–68). Italian furniture and lighting designers. *See:* Mezzadro.

Norman Cherner (1920–87) American furniture designer. *See:* Cherner Chair.

Joe Colombo (1930–71) Italian furniture and product designer. *See:* Elda Chair; Birillo.

Robin Day (1915–) British furniture designer. *See:* Polyprop.

Tom Dixon (1959–) British furniture designer. *See:* S Chair; Bird Chaise Longue.

Charles (1907–78) and **Ray Eames** (1912–88). American furniture designers. *See:* Molded Plywood Chairs (LCW/DCW /DCM/ LCM); La Chaise; LAR, DAR and RAR; DSX, DSW and DSR; Model 670 and Model 671 (Lounge Chair and Ottoman); Soft Pad.

Preben Fabricius (1931–84) and **Jørgen Kastholm** (1931–2007). Danish furniture designers. *See:* Scimitar Chair.

Frank O. Gehry (1929–) American architect and furniture designer. *See:* Easy Edges Series; Power Play Club Chair.

Eileen Gray (1878–1976) Anglo-Irish architect and furniture designer. *See:* Transat; Bibendum Chair.

Matthew Hilton (1957–) British furniture designer. *See:* Balzac Armchair and Ottoman.

Josef Hoffmann (1870–1956) Austrian furniture designer. *See:* Sitzmaschine.

Peter Hvidt (1916–86) and **Orla Mølgaard-Nielsen** (1907–93) Danish architects and furniture designers. *See:* Ax Chair.

Arne Jacobsen (1902–71) Danish architect and furniture designer. *See:* Ant (Model 3100); Model 3107 (Series 7); Egg Chair; Swan Chair; Drop Chair.

Grete Jalk (1920–) Danish furniture designer and architect. *See:* Lounge Chair.

Pierre Jeanneret (1896–1967) Swiss architect and furniture designer. *See:* Chaise Longue LC4; LC2 (Grand Confort).

Finn Juhl (1912–71) Danish furniture designer. *See:* Pelikan; NV-45; Chieftain Chair.

Toshiyuki Kita (1942–) Japanese environmental and industrial designer. *See:* Wink Lounge Chair.

Poul Kjærholm (1929–80) Danish furniture designer. *See:* PK22; PK31 Armchair; PK9; PK24 Chaise Longue.

Kaare Klint (1888–1954) Danish architect and furniture designer. *See:* Faaborg Chair.

Yrjö Kukkapuro (1933–) Finnish furniture designer. *See:* Karuselli Chair.

Shiro Kuramata (1934–1991) Japanese furniture designer. *See:* How High the Moon.

Le Corbusier (born Charles-Édouard Jeanneret-Gris) (1887–1965) Swiss-French architect and furniture designer. *See:* Chaise Longue LC4; LC2 (Grand Confort).

Charles Rennie Mackintosh (1868–1928) Scottish architect and furniture designer. *See:* High Back Chair for Miss Cranston's Tea Rooms.

Bruno Mathsson (1907–88) Swedish furniture designer. *See:* The Grasshopper; Eva Chair.

Ludwig Mies van der Rohe (1886–1969) German architect and furniture designer. *See:* Barcelona Chair; Brno Chair (MR50).

Børge Mogensen (1914–72) Danish furniture designer. *See:* Hunting Chair; Spanish Chair (Model 2226).

Jasper Morrison (1959–) British product and furniture designer. *See:* Thinking Man's Chair, Low Pad.

Olivier Mourgue (1939–) French furniture and landscape designer. *See:* Djinn Chaise Longue.

George Nelson (1908–86) American furniture designer. *See:* MAA (Swag Leg Chair); Coconut Chair.

Marc Newson (1963–) Australian furniture designer. *See:* Lockheed Lounge.

Verner Panton (1926–98) Danish furniture designer. *See:* Cone Chair, Panton Stacking Chair.

Pierre Paulin (1927–2009) French furniture and product designer. *See:* Ribbon Chair.

Charlotte Perriand (1903–99) French architect and furniture designer. *See:* Chaise Longue LC4; LC2 (Grand Confort).

Gio Ponti (1891–1979) Italian architect and furniture designer. *See:* Superleggera.

Jean Prouvé (1901–84) French engineer and designer. *See:* Cité Longue Chair; Antony Chair (Model 356).

Ernest Race (1913–64) British furniture designer. *See*: Antelope Chair.

Lilly Reich (1885–47) German furniture designer. *See*: Barcelona Chair; Brno Chair (MR50).

Gerrit Thomas Rietveld (1888–1964) Dutch architect. *See*: Red/Blue Chair; Zig–Zag Chair.

Eero Saarinen (1910–61) Finnish–American architect and furniture designer. *See*: Womb Chair; Tulip Chair (Model 150).

August Thonet (1829–1910) Austrian furniture designer and manufacturer. *See*: Stuhl Chair (Model 209).

Mart Stam (1899–1986) Dutch architect and furniture designer. *See*: Cantilever Chair (S33).

Philippe Starck (1949–) French architect and product designer. *See*: Louis 20 Chair.

Gerald Summers (1899–1967) British furniture designer. *See*: Armchair.

Poul M. Volther (1923–2001) Danish furniture designer and architect. *See*: Corona Chair.

Ole Wanscher (1903–85) Danish furniture designer. *See*: The Colonial Chair (PJ149).

Hans J. Wegner (1914–2007) Danish furniture designer. *See*: Round Chair (The Chair); Wishbone Chair; Folding Chair (JH512); Flag Halyard; Teddy Bear Chair (PP19); Sawhorse Easy Chair (CH28); Valet Chair (PP250); Cow Horn Chair; Ox Chair; Shell Chair (CH07); The Circle Chair (PP130).

Sori Yanagi (1915–) Japanese furniture designer. *See*: Butterfly Stool.

Marco Zanuso (1916–2001) Italian industrial designer and architect. *See*: Lady Chair.

Index

Acknowledgements

New Holland Publishers would like to thank the following for allowing the use of their images in this book. Every effort has been made to contact copyright holders, but should there be any omissions, the Publishers would be pleased to insert the appropriate acknowledgement in any subsequent printing of this publication.

Picture credits: High Back Chair for Miss Cranston's Tea Room – Charles Rennie Mackintosh: © Culture of Sport, Glasgow (Museums): p.11; Stuhl Chair (Model 209) – August Thonet: Courtesy of Thonet: p.12; Sitzmaschine – Josef Hoffmann: The Bridgeman Art Library/Private Collection: p.15; Faaborg Chair – Kaare Klint: Courtesy of Rudrasmussen: p.16; Red/Blue Chair – Gerrit Thomas Rietveld: Cassina I Maestri Collection/© DACS 2011: pp.7, 19, B3 (Wassily Chair) – Marcel Breuer: Courtesy of Knoll: p.20; Cantilever Chair (S33) – Mart Stam: Courtesy of Thonet: p.23; Transat Chair – Eileen Gray: © Victoria and Albert Museum, London: p.24; Chaise Longue LC4 – Le Corbusier/Jeanneret/Perriand: Cassina/© FLC/ADAGP, Paris and DACS, London 2011: p.27; B32 – Marcel Breuer: DIGITAL IMAGE © 2011, The Museum of Modern Art/Scala, Florence: p.28; LC2 (Grand Confort) Club Chair – Le Corbusier/Jeanneret/Perriand: Cassina/© FLC/ADAGP, Paris and DACS, London 2011: p.31; Bibendum Chair – Eileen Gray: Courtesy of Aram: p.32; Barcelona Chair – Mies van der Rohe/Reich: Courtesy of Knoll: p.35; Brno Chair (MR50) – Mies van der Rohe: DIGITAL IMAGE © 2011, The Museum of Modern Art, New York/Scala, Florence: p.36; Cité Lounge Chair – Jean Prouvé: Courtesy of Aram: p.39; The Grasshopper – Bruno Mathsson: Courtesy of Bruno Mathsson International: p.40; 41 Paimio – Alvar Aalto: Produced by Artek. Courtesy of SCP/© DACS 2011: pp.6, 43; Model No.31 (Cantilever Chair) – Alvar Aalto: Sotheby's/AKG-Images: p.44; Model No.60 (Stacking Stool) – Alvar Aalto: Alamy/V & A Images/© DACS 2011: p.47; Armchair – Gerald Summers: DIGITAL IMAGE © 2011, The Museum of Modern Art, New York/Scala, Florence: p.48; Zig-Zag Chair – Gerrit Thomas Rietveld: Cassina I Maestri Collection/© DACS 2011: p.51; Eva Chair – Bruno Mathsson: Photo courtesy of Wright (www.wright20.com): p.52; Isokon Long Chair – Marcel Breuer: Courtesy of Isokon Plus: p.55; Pelikan Chair – Finn Juhl: Courtesy of One Collection: p.56; NV-45 – Finn Juhl: Courtesy of Skandium: p.59; Moulded Wood Chairs (LCW/DCW/DCM/LCM) – Charles and Ray Eames: Courtesy of Hermann Miller: p.60; Womb Chair – Eero Saarinen: Courtesy of Knoll: p.63; La Chaise – Charles and Ray Eames: Courtesy of Vitra: pp. 8, 64; LAR, DAR and RAR – Charles and Ray Eames: Produced by Modernica. Courtesy of SCP: p.67; Round Chair (The Chair) – Hans J. Wegner: Courtesy of PP Møbler: p.68; Chieftain Chair – Finn Juhl: Courtesy of Skandium: p.71; Wishbone Chair – Hans J. Wegner: Courtesy of Carl Hansen: p.72; The Colonial Chair (PJ 149) – Ole Wanscher: Courtesy of PJ Furniture: p.75; Folding Chair (JH512) – Hans J. Wegner: Courtesy of PP Møbler: p.76; Ax Chair – Hvidt and Mølgaard-Nielsen: Courtesy of Danish Homestore: p.79; Hunting Chair – Børge Mogensen: Courtesy of Lauritz.com : p.80; Flag Halyard (PP 205) – Hans J. Wegner: Courtesy of PP Møbler: p.83; DSX, DSW and DSR – Charles and Ray Eames: Courtesy of Herman Miller: p.84; Teddy Bear Chair (PP19) – Hans J. Wegner: Courtesy of PP Møbler: p.87; Antelope Chair – Ernest Race: Photo courtesy of Wright (www.wright20.com): p.88; Lady Chair – Marco Zanuso: DIGITAL IMAGE © 2011, The Museum of Modern Art, New York/Scala, Florence: p.91; Ant (Model 3100) – Arne Jacobsen: Courtesy of Fritz Hansen: p.92; Sawhorse Easy Chair (CH28) – Hans J. Wegner: Courtesy of Carl Hansen: p.95; Cow Horn Chair (PP 505) – Hans J. Wegner: PP Møbler: p.96; Bird Chair and Ottoman – Harry Bertoia: Courtesy of Knoll/© ARS, NY and DACS, London 2011: p.99; Diamond Chair – Harry Bertoia: Courtesy of Knoll/© ARS, NY and DACS, London 2011: p.100; Valet Chair (PP250) – Hans J. Wegner: Courtesy of PP Møbler: p.103; Antony Chair (Model 356) – Jean Prouvé: Courtesy of Vitra (Hans Hansen): p.104; Butterfly Stool – Sori Yanagi: Produced by Vitra: p.107; Coconut Chair – George Nelson: Courtesy of Herman Miller: p.108; Series 7 chairs – Arne Jacobsen: Courtesy of Cassina: p.111; Tulip (Model 150) – Eero Saarinen: Courtesy of The Conran Shop (www.conranshop.co.uk): p.112; PK22 – Poul Kjærholm: Courtesy of Fritz Hansen: p.115; Model 670 and Model 671 (Lounge Chair and Ottoman) – Charles and Ray Eames: Alamy/V & A Images: p.117; 699 Superleggera – Gio Ponti: Photo courtesy of Wright (www.wright20.com): p.119; Mezzadro – Achille and Pier Giacomo Castiglioni: Courtesy of Zanotta (www.zanotta.it): p.120; Egg Chair – Arne Jacobsen: Courtesy of Fritz Hansen: pp.4, 123; Egg – Nanna Ditzel: Courtesy of Studio Prada (www.studioprada.com): p.124; Swan Chair – Arne Jacobsen: Courtesy of Fritz Hansen: p.127; Cherner Chair – Norman Cherner: Courtesy of Cherner Chair Company: p.128; MAA (Swag Leg Chair) – George Nelson: Courtesy of Herman Miller: p.131; PK31 Armchair – Poul Kjærholm: Courtesy of Fritz Hansen: p.132; Cone Chair – Verner Panton: Courtesy of Knoll: p.135; Drop Chair – Arne Jacobsen: Courtesy of 1st Dibs/Almond Hartzog (www.1stdibs.com): p.136; Spanish Chair (Model 2226) – Børge Mogensen: Courtesy of Fredericia Furniture (www.frederica.com): p.139; Ox Chair – Hans J. Wegner: Courtesy of Erik Jørgensen: p.140; PK9 – Poul Kjærholm: Courtesy of Fritz Hansen: p.143; Corona Chair (EJ65) – Poul M. Volther: Courtesy of Erik Jørgensen: p.144; Polyprop – Robin Day: Courtesy of Hille: p.147; Scimitar Chair – Fabricus and Kastholm: Courtesy PBA Auctions (www.pba-auctions.com): p.148; Shell Chair (CH07) – Hans J. Wegner: Photo courtesy of Carl Hansen: p.151; Lounge Chair – Greta Jalk: DIGITAL IMAGE © 2011, The Museum of Modern Art, New York/Scala, Florence: p.152; Djinn Chaise Longue – Olivier Mourgue: DIGITAL IMAGE © 2011, The Museum of Modern Art, New York/Scala, Florence: p.155; Karuselli Chair – Yrjö Kukkapuro: Courtesy of The Conran Shop (www.conranshop.com): p.156; Elda Chair – Joe Colombo: Courtesy of Longhi (www.longhi.it): p.159; Ribbon Chair – Pierre Paulin: Courtesy of Artifort (www.artifort.com): p.160; Ball (Globe) Chair – Eero Aarnio: Courtesy of Adelta (www.adelta): p.163; PK24 Chaise Longue (Hammock) – Poul Kjærholm: Courtesy of Fritz Hansen: p.164; Panton Stacking Chair – Verner Panton: Courtesy of Vitra: 167; Bubble Chair – Eero Aarnio: Courtesy of Adelta: (www.adelta): p.168; Soft Pad – Charles and Ray Eames: Courtesy of Herman Miller: p.171; Birillo – Joe Colombo: Photo courtesy of Wright (www.wight20.com): p.172; Easy Edges Series – Frank O. Gehry: Bridgeman Art Library/Gift of Suzanne Labiner to American Friends of the Israel Museum: p.175; Wink Lounge Chair – Toshiyuki Kita: Cassina I Contemporanei Collection: p.176; Rover Chair – Ron Arad: Courtesy of Ron Arad Associates: p.179; Seconda 602 – Mario Botta: Courtesy Mario Botta www.botta.ch (Photographer Aldo Ballo): p.180; The Circle Chair (PP 130) – Hans J. Wegner: Courtesy of PP Møbler (www.ppdk.com): p.183; Lockheed Lounge – Marc Newson: Courtesy of Marc Newson (www.marc-newson.com) (Photographer Carin Katt): p.184; How High the Moon – Shiro Kuramata: DIGITAL IMAGE © 2011, The Museum of Modern Art, New York/Scala, Florence: p.187; Thinking Man's Chair – Jasper Morrison: By Cappellini. Available at SCP (www.scp.co.uk) t.0207 739 1869: p.187; S Chair – Tom Dixon: Courtesy of Cappellini: p.191; Power Play Club Chair – Frank O. Gehry: Courtesy of Knoll: p.192; Louis 20 Chair – Philippe Stark: Photograph courtesy of Machine Age, Boston, MA (Photographer: Norman Mainville) : p.195; Balzac Armchair and Ottoman – Matthew Hilton: Courtesy of Heals (www.heals.co.uk): p.196; Bird Chaise Longue – Tom Dixon: Courtesy of Cappellini: p.199; Low Pad – Jasper Morrison: Courtesy of Cappellini: p.200.